18919

DATE DUE

FEB '87			
MR 24 '87			
NOV 25 '92			
JAN 27 '93			
FEB 15 '00			
SEP 2 0 2006			

THE WALTER LYNWOOD FLEMING
LECTURES IN SOUTHERN HISTORY

LOUISIANA STATE UNIVERSITY

Plain Folk
of the Old South

By
FRANK LAWRENCE
OWSLEY

With a new Introduction by
Grady McWhiney

LOUISIANA
STATE UNIVERSITY PRESS

BATON ROUGE AND LONDON

Library of Congress Cataloging in Publication Data

Owsley, Frank Lawrence, 1890–1956.
Plain folk of the Old South.

Reprint. Originally published: Baton Rouge:
Louisiana State University Press, 1949. (The
Walter Lynwood Fleming lectures in southern
history)
  Includes bibliographical references and index.
  1. Southern States—Social life and customs—1775–
1865. 2. Southern States—History—1775–1865.
I. Title. II. Series: Walter Lynwood Fleming
lectures in southern history.
F213.094   1982   975'.03   82-9903
ISBN 0-8071-1062-0   AACR2
ISBN 0-8071-1063-9 (pbk.)

To
Margaret and Larry
this volume is
lovingly dedicated

Introduction

Some books deserve a long and influential life. One of these is Frank S. Owsley's *Plain Folk of the Old South*, first published in 1949 by Louisiana State University Press. In 1965, when this work was no longer readily available, I persuaded the people at Quadrangle Books to publish it as an inexpensive paperback. Since that edition has been out of print for some time, plans by the LSU Press to reissue *Plain Folk* came as a delightful surprise.

Each reading of *Plain Folk* increases both my admiration for its author and my conviction that this is one of the most important books on the South ever written. No previous work explained the nature of antebellum southern society as well. Southerners were, as Owsley so effectively shows, a rural people with rural values whose society was far more complex than the simplistic, yet persistent, stereotype of the Old South. Instead of the hoary division of the agricultural population into slaves, slaveowners, and nonslaveowning poor whites, Owsley found a rich diversity: slaveholders owning various amounts of land, nonslaveholders with many or few acres, landless renters with or without slaves, squatters, farm laborers, and "a 'leisure class' whose means of support do not appear on the record." Owsley concluded that "the core of the social structure was a massive body of plain folk who were neither rich nor very poor. These were employed in numerous occupations; but the great majority secured their food, clothing, and shelter from some rural pursuit, chiefly farming and livestock grazing" (pp. 7–8).

Owsley made no claim to discovering the southern plain folk, but he and his wife, Harriet Chappell Owsley, and his students were the first to use the manuscript census reports and other neglected sources—wills, county-court minutes, marriage licenses, church records, inventory of estates, trial records, mortgage books, deed books, tax records, as well as travel accounts and local histories—to recreate the society of the antebellum South.

A revealing glimpse of his research methods and of how Owsley viewed his work is found in a letter he wrote to Charles A. Beard in 1940, just after the *Journal of Southern History* published "The Economic Basis of Society in the Late Ante-Bellum South," coauthored by Owsley and his wife:

> We have, I guess, obtained the micro-film copies of 50,000 pages of the unpublished census reports and the county tax books for the late ante bellum period, and for Georgia, fortunately, we have the tax books for many representative counties that go back to the American Revolution. These records cover South Carolina, Georgia, Florida, Tennessee, Alabama, Mississippi and Louisiana. At first, in our innocence, Mrs. Owsley and I set out to analyze all this data ourselves; and you may judge of the speed possible in such an undertaking when I tell you that the figures used in the article we sent you were the results of an entire year's work of both of us.

Owsley noted that he had assigned "*mature graduate* students" to study other states. Their findings, he reported,

> presents a picture that is completely at variance with the accepted one: Hardly a single family failed to ascend the economic ladder. Non slave holders increased their holdings, increased their crop productions, increased the value and breed apparently of their live

stock. Many who were landless in 1850 became land owners and even slave owners in 1860. Indeed so many of the non slave holders of 1850 became slave holders by 1860 that it materially colors and affects any analysis based upon the classification of "slave holder" and non "slave holder" unless the shift of the non slave holder to the slave holder class is taken into account. All this took place in the face of the incredible and unrealistic price of slaves, which, it seems, to me, to point to other factors besides slavery, as the sources of this prosperity: cheap and good land, improved methods of agriculture, improved breeds of cattle, good but not high prices for farm produce and live stock sold, reasonable prices for things purchased by the farmers.[1]

Professional historians often were both dazzled and disturbed by the findings of Owsley and his students. Most reviewers of *Plain Folk* were impressed by its fresh and important conclusions, but they were hesitant to accept all that was offered. Some of what Owsley said was simply too startling: that small farmers were not driven from the best agricultural lands by slaveowning planters; that the plain folk "lived dispersed over all the arable regions of the South and were settled in considerable numbers on every type of soil adapted to agricultural uses" (pp. 51–52); that in the lower South "from 80 to 85 per cent of the agricultural population owned their land" (p. 16); that the "opportunity of acquiring land was greater in the South than in the North" (p. 17); and that it was "agriculture rather than slavery that pressed . . . settlers into the less fertile and more rugged lands" (p. 34).

Plain Folk superseded much of the vast and elaborate literature devoted to how slavery and the plantation system supposedly dominated the Old South. If Owsley's conclusions were correct, much of what previously had been written

[1] Frank L. Owsley to Charles A. Beard, October 12, 1940 (copy furnished by Harriet Chappell Owsley).

about the South was no longer valid and the whole history of the region would have to be reexamined. Cautious scholars, some with vested interests in the old interpretations, were reluctant to give Owsley's findings their full support. A typical reviewer claimed that *Plain Folk* "does not destroy—as it sometimes seems to imply it does—the equally valid fact that slavery and the plantation dominated the institutional structure of very large portions of the older settled regions." Another reviewer insisted that Owsley "has failed to destroy the fact that slavery and the plantation system completely dominated the area." More perceptive scholars, such as Clement Eaton, spoke of the "major contributions to southern history" made by Owsley, and Charles A. Beard thought that Owsley's studies should "be extended all over the country, for they alone can provide a solid base for discovering the status of agricultural economy at given periods."[2]

One of the greatest strengths of *Plain Folk* is its sympathetic understanding of southern rural life. Owsley paid close attention to migration and settlement patterns. He discovered that most of the people who settled the lower South were from the Carolina backcountry (p. 68). Many were self-sufficient and restless herdsmen who grazed their livestock on the open range. "The herdsmen were a large and important element of the plain folk of the Old South," concluded Owsley (p. 24). "Livestock grazing was a major occupation in the South" (p. 27); indeed, the grazing of livestock "was of greater relative importance in the antebellum South than in any other part of the United States" (p. 48). Although

---

[2] Robin M. Williams, Jr., in *Social Forces*, XXVIII, 449; Frank F. White, Jr., in *Maryland Historical Magazine*, XLVI, 312; Clement Eaton in *American Historical Review*, LV, 617; Charles A. Beard to Frank L. Owsley, January 15, 1942 (copy furnished by Harriet Chappell Owsley).

influenced by Frederick Jackson Turner's frontier thesis, Owsley perceived that open-range herding not only shaped southern migration and settlement patterns but remained a central part of southern agricultural activity throughout the antebellum period. His description of the herdsmen is classic. Owsley recognized that they were not poor whites (p. 36), but instead leisure-oriented individuals who had little inclination toward hard work, farmed haphazardly, and allowed their free-ranging livestock to make their living for them.

Some of Owsley's most charming observations relate to the extended southern family, which was cohesive and clannish, but "not patriarchal in the European or oriental sense" (p. 94). Owsley wrote with freshness and nostalgia about family life in the Old South and affectionately described amusements, delicious country food, and religious devotion. He acknowledged that there were rowdies, drunkards, and reprobates among the plain folk (p. 103), but his emphasis was upon the more idyllic aspects of life He contended that

> The rural environment of the Old South, where the whole family worked together, hunted together, went to church and parties together, and expected to be buried together and to come to judgment together on the Last Day, helps explain the closely knit family group. Certainly it helps explain the deference of younger persons to their parents and elders, for daily association demonstrated that "pa" knew the seasons, the habits and peculiarities of the crops; that he was a master of woodcraft, and he knew the stratagems of the chase and many other fascinating matters that only long experience and reflection could teach. "Pa" could also cut a smarter step in the reel and square dance and play the fiddle better than the boys could, and they knew it. As for "ma," it would take a lot of hard apprenticeship for the daughters to learn to cook, quilt, knit, garden, and "manage" like she could. As likely as not, too, she could dance forty different square-dance figures—and call them. In other words pa's and ma's opinions

were respected because they demonstrated in their day-long work with their sons and daughters in field and house and in their play that skill and wisdom come from experience. (p. 95)

Without having access to many personal letters and diaries, Owsley managed to recreate the life-style of individuals, families, and communities by using instead such documents as "grand-jury reports, trial records, court minutes, and wills" (p. 18). He discovered that the overwhelming majority of southerners were neither class-conscious in the Marxian sense nor dominated and coerced by large planters; in fact, the plain folk of the Old South enjoyed a remarkable amount of political, social, and economic opportunity and independence (p. 139). To the ambitious white male, southern society was an open door. "Relatively few of the plain folk, however, seem to have had a desire to become wealthy," noted Owsley (p. 134). Their lack of materialism was in marked contrast to that of most nonsoutherners. Owsley's plain folk made little distinction between work and play; they delighted in singing, dancing, and music and were particularly adept at riding, hunting, and fishing. Everybody—men, women, and children—rode, and most males were expert marksmen. The plain folk were a cordial and hospitable people who enjoyed life; few were very wealthy, but even fewer were poor enough actually to suffer want (pp. 104–31).

The distinctiveness of southerners is a strong theme of *Plain Folk*. "Fat or lean, blond or brunet, the Southern type could be discerned by travelers from abroad and from other parts of America," insisted Owsley. "Appearance, the indefinable qualities of personality, and their manners and customs, particularly their distinctive speech, set them apart from the inhabitants of the other sections of the United States, and in this way strengthened their sense of kinship"

(p. 91). That sense of kinship was so strong, Owsley believed, that the "Southern people . . . were a genuine folk long before the Civil War. Even the Southern aristocracy . . . were folkish in their manners and customs and shared to a marked degree in this sense of solidarity." What unified them most was the "common national origin of the bulk of the people" (p. 90). It is here, with unusual insight, that Owsley came so very close to identifying the cultural ethnicity of southerners when he wrote: "The closely knit family with its ramified and widespreading kinship ties was a folk characteristic which the Southerners possessed to a degree second only to the Highland Scots of an earlier time" (p. 94).

One of Owsley's most significant yet often overlooked points was that cultural conservatism shaped the Old South. The plain folk were bound by traditions and culturally conditioned to settle in country similar to that where they came from; they rarely varied from their accustomed activities and folkways (pp. 52–55). In his emphasis upon culture rather than economics as the primary determinant, Owsley departed from the fashionable trend in the historiography of his time. "Your findings thus far are certainly astonishing," Charles A. Beard, the historian most associated with the economic interpretation of American history, confessed to Owsley in 1940. Beard admitted that the cultural influences described by Owsley were impressive, expressed his desire to "have a good talk" with Owsley, and then asked: "Do you know Professor [Richard] Shyrock at Pennsylvania University? If not, you should, for he has thought a lot about cultural determinism as against economic determinism, and strikes fire with his flint and steel."[3]

[3] Charles A. Beard to Frank L. Owsley, October 20 [1940] (copy furnished by Harriet Chappell Owsley). See Richard H. Shyrock, "British Versus German Traditions in Colonial Agriculture," *Mississippi*

In yet another way Owsley differed from the usual historian. He was not ashamed of the South. He was proud of his Alabama origins and southern ancestry. In 1930 he boldly joined some of his Vanderbilt University colleagues to defend the South and an agrarian way of life against the forces of modernism and industrialism.[4] About this time, Harriet Owsley recalled, her husband "became increasingly aware that the currently-accepted interpretation of the South and its history had no basis of fact. The histories of the region had been written almost altogether by Northerners who had never been in the South and they were based on assumptions which had not been thoroughly tested. With this discovery his sense of scholarly integrity and historical justice was aroused, and from that time until his death, he considered it his mission in life to correct these misconceptions."[5]

His defense of southern and agrarian ways, combined with his attempt to protect the South's history from distortion, brought down upon Owsley the full wrath of certain nationalistic historians. In 1956 he explained what happened after he and his fellow Agrarians began writing in defense of the South:

> I was very much aware of a crusade being levelled against the South. I think we all had the same feeling, that not only were we trying to reassert values that we thought were basic, but values that also had a considerable bit of sectional nature. That is, the attack was sectional. . . . We became, I think, in our writings

---

Valley Historical Review, XXVI, 39–54, and Richard H. Shyrock, "Cultural Factors in the History of the South," *Journal of Southern History*, V, 333–46.

[4] Twelve Southerners, *I'll Take My Stand* (New York, 1930), 61–91.

[5] Harriet Chappell Owsley (ed.), *The South: Old and New Frontiers; Selected Essays of Frank Lawrence Owsley* (Athens, Ga., 1969), xvi.

very deliberately provocative. I certainly did, and I have been confronted with it from that time until now by the purists in my profession. In fact, there was a book written last year . . . in which I was spoken of as a "modern fire-eater."[6]

By openly admitting that he was a "southern" historian, Owsley broke with another tradition—the view that still prevails in most graduate schools that historians should be totally detached from their subjects. Owsley had enough sense and courage to reject this worthwhile-sounding but generally impossible and often hypocritical view and to substitute for it a more forthright and a less presumptious approach. "A Southern historian is, I suppose, as objective and impartial as a Northern historian," reasoned Owsley.

Every good historian tries to tell the truth. But historians are human, and, Northern or Southern, they are bound to have emotional reactions to every human situation, no matter how much they try to exercise self-restraint. When emotion is too much in the ascendancy, the historian may be accused of bias, sometimes more elegantly spoken of as "point of view." Facts are supposed to be facts, but they have a queer way of arranging themselves so that one historian may see them one way, another historian another way. Some facts which seem obscure and dim to one may shine clear and bright to another. No one sees them all in their true, clear light.[7]

Frank Owsley was much like the plain folk he described. "He was one of the nicest persons I ever met," remembered a lady. "He was open and straightforward. He was full of delightful little country tales."[8] A historian who was Owsley's colleague at the University of Alabama stated: "He was well-

[6] *Ibid.*, xvii.
[7] *Ibid.*, 223.
[8] Interview with Nina Hall Doster, November 4, 1981.

named; he was very 'Frank.' "[9] Another professor who knew Owsley described him as

> warm and friendly. He stayed late in the archives. He laughed easily. On his feet, he could say the right things; his ad lib remarks were great! The man could have been a fine orator. He never harbored grudges, and took criticism with good humor. He always asked young people what they were doing, and he had time for graduate students. His manner was gracious and hospitable. He told excellent stories. An outstanding critic, he nevertheless was kind to everyone. He took off on the history snobs and the pretentious big shots. Always open-minded, he never said he had the answers. He and Harriet were a great team. He had the imagination in teaching that a great novelist had in writing.[10]

Critics of Owsley and his work have been more assertive than assiduous, more willing to challenge him than to prove him wrong. It was easy enough to claim, as did University of North Carolina graduate student Fabian Linden in a frequently cited article, that the studies of Owsley and his students "were found to be statistically unrepresentative," or that most of Owsley's conclusions were wrong, but such assertions remain unproven.[11] Critics have failed to follow up their challenges with solid research; no systematic refutation of *Plain Folk* has appeared in the thirty-three years since it was first published. Perhaps this is because most of Owsley's conclusions are valid. It would be disappointing to discover,

[9] Interview with James F. Doster, November 4, 1981.

[10] Interview with Bennett H. Wall, April 21, 1981.

[11] Fabian Linden, "Economic Democracy in the Slave South," *Journal of Negro History*, XXXI, 140–89. A North Carolina sociologist asserted that "Professor Owsley . . . is much too innocent of the use and resources of modern statistical method" and his "analysis has not been carried through to completion." Rupert B. Vance in *Journal of Southern History*, XVI, 547.

after the expenditure of much time and energy, that what one had hoped to disprove was correct after all.

If many of the statements made by Owsley in *Plain Folk* seem less than startling today, it is because they have become part of the generally accepted interpretation of southern history. It is a tribute to Frank Owsley—his insight and his research—that so many of his discoveries still inform and shape the history of the South.

GRADY MCWHINEY

University of Alabama
March, 1982

Foreword

THE TITLE of this volume, *The Plain Folk of the Old South*, could well have been "The Forgotten Man of the Old South," for this is the subject which I have pursued, perhaps a bit relentlessly, from the first to the last page. I have chosen a less flamboyant title, however, because it is in keeping with the common people's conception of themselves. They thought of themselves as plain folk, except they would have said "plain folks," and they would have had pride in their self-description; for to them it connoted the sum of the solid virtues—integrity, independence, self-respect, courage, love of freedom, love of their fellow man, and love of God. The plain folk, as I have emphasized throughout this volume, were usually landowning farmers and herdsmen, though a small minority were engaged exclusively in other occupations. Their thoughts, traditions, and legends were rural, for with the exception of an occasional ancestor who had been brought from some British city or debtor's prison as an indentured servant, their family trees were rooted in the soil. Their forebears in the British Isles, and in France and Germany, had been yeomen and peasant farmers since before the dawn of recorded history. To them the land was, with God's blessings, the direct source of all the necessities of life and of all material riches.

Because of the great increase in population, together

with the enclosure acts and other similar monopolistic trends, the freeholds and leaseholds of the yeomen farmers of Western Europe, especially Great Britain and Ireland, became too small for comfortable support and in many cases too small to furnish subsistence. These farmers thus crowded upon inadequate holdings, and often deprived of access to the land, were in consequence possessed of a great land hunger. In America, and especially in the South, they found a boundless domain which, together with a genial climate, they came to regard as theirs by the manifest will of the Divine Providence. Though many settled as landless tenants or migrated from one frontier to another as squatters and lived by hunting and grazing cattle, the majority of these rural emigrants and their descendants acquired freeholds. Indeed, as I have suggested frequently in the following pages, from their ranks came numerous large landowners and slaveholders and a substantial portion of those in the learned professions. But the greater part remained landowning farmers who belonged neither to the plantation economy nor to the destitute and frequently degraded poor-white class. They, and not the poor whites, comprised the bulk of the Southern population from the Revolution to the Civil War.

Since, in the writing of our history, the plain folk of the Old South have been so long relegated either to obscurity or to oblivion, it has been a task closely akin to archaeology to recover them. But granted that a large fraction of these folk have been historically exhumed in this and other recent studies, some of which are cited in this volume, they are still in danger of being reinterred. There is a conflict between their reality and importance and the vested interests of written history. Much of the history of this great country has been written upon assumptions which have never been thoroughly tested, and the nonexistence of a large rural middle class in the Old South is, perhaps, the most important assumption of them all. Indeed, volumes and shelves of history treating of the antebellum period and in which causes of the Civil War are traced, assume that there were only three important classes in the South—planters, Negro slaves, and poor whites. Nor will the Marxian formula for human behavior and history find a place for a middle class as such records as the census and tax lists reveal statistically.

At this point I should like to explain that the first four chapters of this book, in an abbreviated form, were delivered at Louisiana State University as the "Walter Lynwood Fleming Lectures in Southern History" (1948). Chapter V, dealing with a statistical analysis of landownership and slaveholding, was of course not given as a lecture, but by the courtesy of the Louisiana State University Press was included as a necessary reference. The generosity of the publishers permitted further infringements of the customary format of the "Fleming Lectures" by the inclusion of an index and footnotes. I did not, however, think that a formal bibliography was necessary in view of the fact that a discussion of methodology and source material forms no inconsiderable portion of the text itself.

At the risk of repeating what is stated elsewhere. I should like to say that the sampling method has been used in the statistical foundation of this work—and in articles on the subject published by myself and my wife, Harriet C. Owsley. Complete studies for the late antebellum period were made of representative counties in the states selected. Furthermore, these states were, with the exception of Tennessee, from the Lower South. The upper seaboard states of the Old South are in the process of being studied by my graduate students, and the findings are not vastly different from those presented here and in the other studies referred to in this work. This, of course, means that in certain matters, one may speak of the entire Old South with more authority than has been revealed in the footnotes.

As in former publications, my wife is essentially the joint author of this book. She has constantly aided in the research for this volume and for other projected works on this subject which, it is hoped, may appear from time to time. In this particular volume she made the statistical analysis, prepared the land maps, and made the Index.

I wish to express my gratitude to the Social Science Research Council, to the Carnegie Fund, and to the Institute for Research and Training in the Social Sciences at Vanderbilt University for grants-in-aid for the furtherance of work on this and related subjects. The staffs of Vanderbilt University Library, Duke University Library, the Departments of Archives and History of Alabama, Georgia, and Tennessee, and the Bureau of Census, Washington, D.C., have aided greatly in collecting materials for this work. Valuable assistance has been rendered by the officers of the numerous counties in Georgia, Alabama, and Tennessee visited by the author. Acknowledgment is also made to Dr. Herbert Weaver and Dr. Harry T. Coles for the use of their respective works on Mississippi and Louisiana referred to in this volume.

FRANK LAWRENCE OWSLEY

University of Alabama
June 13, 1949

Contents

Maps

Tables

Plain Folk
of the Old South

Chapter I

Southern Society:
A Reinterpretation

MOST TRAVELERS and critics who wrote about the South during the late antebellum period were of the opinion that the white inhabitants of the South generally fell into two categories, namely, the slaveholders and the "poor whites." Moreover, whether or not they intended to do so, they created the impression in the popular mind that the slaveholder was a great planter living in a white-columned mansion, attended by a squad of Negro slaves who obsequiously attended his every want and whim. According to the opinion of such writers, these "cavaliers" were the great monopolists of their day; they crowded everyone not possessed of considerable wealth off the good lands and even the lands from which modest profits might be realized; they dominated politics, religion, and all phases of public life. The six or seven million nonslaveholders who comprised the remainder of the white population and were, with minor exceptions, considered "poor whites" or "poor white trash" were visualized as a sorry lot indeed. They had been pushed off by the planters into the pine barrens and sterile sand hills and mountains. Here as squatters upon abandoned lands and government tracts they dwelt in squalid log huts and kept alive by hunting and fishing, and by growing patches of corn, sweet potatoes, collards, and pumpkins in the small "deadenings" or clearings they had made in the all-engulfing wilderness. They were illiterate, shiftless, irresponsible, frequently vicious, and nearly always addicted to the use of "rot gut" whiskey and to dirt eating. Many, perhaps nearly all, according to later writers, had malaria, hookworm, and pellagra. Between the Great Unwashed and the slaveholders there was a chasm that could not be bridged. The nonslaveholders were six or seven million supernumeraries in a slaveholding society.[1]

Frederick Law Olmsted, perhaps, contributed more than any other writer to the version of Southern society sketched above; for he was possessed of unusual skill in the art of reporting detail and of completely wiping out the validity of such detail by subjective comments and generalizations. For example, despite the fact that he saw little destitution and almost constant evidence of well-being among the poorer folk, he was still able to conclude "that the majority of the Negroes at the North live more comfortably than the majority of whites at the South"; that, indeed, the majority of the people of the South were poor whites. It was not, in his opinion, sterile soil and unhealthful climate that created the great mass of poor whites, but slavery. These people would not work because work was identified with slavery, "For manual agricultural labor . . . ," Olmsted wrote, "the free man looking on, has a contempt, and for its necessity in himself, if such necessity exists, a pity quite beyond that of the man under

---

[1] See A. J. N. Den Hollander, "The Tradition of the Poor White" in W. T. Couch (ed.), *Culture in the South* (Chapel Hill, 1934), 403, 415, for a criticism of the traditional view of society in the antebellum South.

whose observations it has been free from such an association of ideas." Olmsted could make this generalization despite the fact that throughout his extensive travels in the South he had constantly observed Negro slaves and whites working in the fields together. Indeed, the degradation of free labor by slavery was Olmsted's major premise from which all conclusions flowed regardless of the factual observations that he conscientiously incorporated in his books.[2]

Other writers, who had little or no firsthand knowledge of the South, quite naturally relied on the writings of travelers, and particularly Olmsted, who was regarded as dispassionate and authoritative. Their tendency was to seize upon the generalizations rather than the detailed reporting of the travel literature, with the result that they further simplified the picture of Southern society. George M. Weston's *Poor Whites of the South* and his *Progress of Slavery in the United States* are excellent examples of this process of simplification. "The whites of the South not connected with the ownership or management of slaves," he wrote, "constituting not far from three fourths of the whole number of whites, confined at least to the low wages of agricultural labor, and partly cut off even from this by the degradation of a companionship with black slaves, retire to the outskirts of civilization, where they lead a semisavage life, sinking deeper and more hopelessly into barbarism with each succeeding generation. The slave owner takes at first all the best lands, and finally all the lands susceptible of regular cultivation; and the poor whites, thrown back

[2] Frederick L. Olmsted, *A Journey in the Back Country* (New York, 1863), 237, 297, 298, 299, *passim*. See also *id.*, *A Journey in the Seaboard Slave States, with Remarks on Their Economy* (New York, 1856), and *A Journey Through Texas* (New York, 1857), *passim*.

upon the hills and upon the sterile soils—[are] mere squatters without energy enough to acquire the title even to the cheap lands they occupy, without roads, and at length, without even a desire for education. . . ." [3]

J. E. Cairnes, the British economist, presented the final stereotype of Southern society in his book *The Slave Power*. Cairnes appears to have rested his generalizations about the social structure of the South largely upon those of Olmsted, Weston, and Hinton Rowen Helper. It was a pyramid upon a pyramid. But it was a picture of Southern society that made a deep and lasting impression, for as late as 1947 Allan Nevins drew upon Cairnes's *Slave Power* in his *Ordeal of the Union*. "The constitution of a slave society . . . resolves itself into three classes," writes Cairnes, "broadly distinguished from each other and connected by no common interest—the slaves on whom devolves all the regular industry, the slaveholders who reap all its fruits, and an idle and lawless rabble who live dispersed over vast plains in a condition little removed from absolute barbarism." [4] "These mean whites . . . are the natural growth of the slave system"; "regular industry is only known to them as the vocation of slaves, and it is the one fate which above all others they desire to avoid." [5] "In the Southern States no less than five million human beings [who have been expelled from the good lands by the slaveholders] are now said to exist . . . in a condition little removed from savage life, eking out a wretched subsistence by hunting, fishing, by hiring themselves out for occasional jobs, by plunder." [6]

---

[3] George M. Weston, *The Poor Whites of the South* (Washington, 1856), 5. His *Progress of Slavery* was published in 1857.

[4] J. E. Cairnes, *The Slave Power: Its Character, Career and Probable Designs* (New York, 1862), 60.

[5] *Ibid.*, 78, 79.

[6] *Ibid.*, 54.

The generalization that these writers made about the Old South—which may well be considered the first version of *Tobacco Road*—should be kept in mind, for they have been subjected to frequent examination in preparing this study and will be points of reference in it.

A few Southern historians have accepted in whole or in part the picture of the society of the Old South, as portrayed by such writers as those quoted previously; but most of them, without doubt, have regarded it as fantastic. Sometimes with an expression of indignation on their faces they will say "folks are just not like that in the South. Society is not and never has been divided into rich and poor." Those who were born before 1890 had a firsthand acquaintance with one and often two generations who had lived before 1860 and who were not—nor had they ever been—either poor whites or planters. For example, outstanding Southern historians such as J. G. de Roulhac Hamilton, Charles W. Ramsdell, George Petrie, and Walter Lynwood Fleming grew up in communities where heads of many families, including their own, had been reared before 1860. It will, perhaps, drive home the idea as to how well antebellum Southern society was known by those born prior to the close of the last century if it is remarked that Confederate soldiers in 1900 were about the average age of veterans of World War I in 1949.

Possessed of this firsthand acquaintance with numerous representatives of the Old South, Southern historians have, with few exceptions up until this time, strongly maintained that the white people of the antebellum rural South were not divided into the simple categories of rich planter and poor white. As time has passed, and with it the older generations, even stronger assertions are being made concerning the plain folk of the Old South and, indeed, concerning the whole society in that region. The tone of some of these claims, as I have suggested, is somewhat indignant just as the tone of anyone tends to grow indignant when he knows from his own observations and experiences whereof he speaks, but discovers that his star witnesses have disappeared from the court. The truth of the matter is that for good reasons, such as a lack of trained historians in the South until well after the opening of the present century, the testimony of these star witnesses, the survivors of the old regime, was not taken while they were numerous enough and young enough for their evidence to be both full and valid. It has been assumed, too, quite naturally, that since the farmers and small planters, unlike the large planters and businessmen, seldom preserved their private papers and business accounts, no record of their manner of life and their place in the Southern society remained after they passed on.

But these millions of people did leave records of their lives: the church records, wills, administration of estates, county-court minutes, marriage licenses, inventory of estates, trial records, mortgage books, deed books, county tax books, and the manuscript returns of the Federal censuses. Other important sources from which much can be learned not only about the plain folk, but about society as a whole in the South, are the older county and town histories, biographies, autobiographies, and recollections of men and women of only local importance—preachers, lawyers, doctors, county newspaper editors, and the like, who knew every family in the county and frequently in a much wider area. Last but not least must be mentioned the writings of those sojourners in the South, who remained in one place long enough to become acquainted with the country and the people. Out of such documents a picture of the whole people can be constructed, not just that of the great planter and merchant, but, in the words of an old jingle: "Rich man, poor man, beggar man, thief, doctor, lawyer, merchant, chief. . . ."

Of all these sources, the county records and the unpublished census reports, which are made by county for each individual, are the most valuable documents from which to study the life of the people as a whole. It is only by employing them in great volume, however, and receiving a cumulative effect that they can at all be usefully employed.

Upon reading page after page of tax lists and census returns, both of which give the landholdings and much of the personal property of all individuals, the picture of the economic structure of the Old South gradually takes form. These sources reveal the existence of a society of great complexity. Instead of the simple, two-fold division of the agricultural population into slaveholders and nonslaveholding poor whites, many economic groups appear. Among the slaveholders there were great planters possessed of thousands of acres of land and hundreds of slaves, planters owning a thousand or fewer acres and two score slaves, small planters with five hundred acres and ten or fifteen slaves, large farmers with three or four hundred acres and five to ten slaves, small farmers with two hundred or fewer acres and one or two slaves. Among the nonslaveholders were large farmers employing hired labor who owned from two hundred to a thousand acres; a middle group which owned from one hundred to two hundred acres; "one horse farmers" with less than one hundred acres; and landless renters, squatters, farm laborers, and a "leisure class" whose means of support does not appear on the record. But the core of the social structure was a massive body of plain folk who were neither rich nor very poor. These were employed in numerous occupations; but the great majority secured their food, clothing, and shelter from some rural pursuit, chiefly farming and livestock grazing. It is the plain country folk with whom I am most concerned here—that great mass of several millions who were not part of the plantation economy. The group included the small slaveholding farmers; the nonslaveholders who owned the land which they cultivated; the numerous herdsmen on the frontier, pine barrens, and mountains; and those tenant farmers whose agricultural production, as recorded in the census, indicated thrift, energy, and self-respect.

It is impossible to convey the picture thus formed by comprehensive examination of tax lists and census reports to those who have not scrutinized these documents to some extent; but, as is so often true under such circumstances, it becomes necessary to resort to abstractions. In this case that means, of course, a statistical analysis, which will be presented later. Only general conclusions and a few sample exhibits from the census reports will be presented here concerning the extent of slave ownings and the spread and sizes of the landholdings of both slaveholders and nonslaveholders.

The slaveholding families composed nearly one third of the white population of the South, and most of them were small slaveowners and small landowners. As estimated, 60 per cent owned from one to five slaves, and another large group held from five to ten. Most slaveholders whose chief occupation was agriculture owned their farms, and the small slaveholders, as would be expected, were small landowners. At least 60 per cent of the small slaveholders had farms ranging in size from fifty to three hundred acres. Over 60 per cent of the nonslaveholders outside the upper seaboard states—who, it will be recalled, were classed as poor white trash—were also landowners. In the lower South and in portions of the upper south central states an estimated 70 per cent owned farms. The sizes of their holdings differed very little from those of the small slaveholders. About 75 per cent ranged from a few to two hundred acres, and the other 25 per cent were above two hundred acres in size. The following tables (I–V inclusive) from the agricultural census returns, with data from the slave schedule added, are examples of the type of material used in making the statistical analyses of land and slave ownership. These tables consist of heads of families engaged in agriculture together with their slaves and landholdings. They were transcribed from Schedule IV (Productions of Agriculture) in the exact order as written in the manuscript census returns of 1850 and 1860. The slaves were added from Schedule II (Slave Inhabitants). The vast data on the census sheets, relating to the agricultural productions, the livestock, slaughtered animals, and home manufactures of each farm operator, had to be omitted because of the impracticability of devising a chart large enough for such data and not too large for use in this volume. Each table represents, in a general way, a rural community or settlement; for the census enumerator usually listed each farm and plantation as he came to it, riding horseback along a neighborhood road. These charts are not intended to be used for any mathematical analysis—that matter has been reserved for the final chapter in this volume—but they are placed at this point to convey a general picture of the social and economic structure of a rural community, and to serve as an introduction to the type of material on which all statistical matter relating to the ownership of land and slaves has been based. The sizes of farms and plantations and of slaveholdings can be seen at a glance to have been more

modest in the rich land areas than tradition has it; and outside the delta the same hasty glance reveals the thorough
intermingling of small and large slaveholders and of all
slaveholders and nonslaveholders. These factors, in the very
beginning, cast doubt upon the validity of the old stereotype of a white society made up of rich planters and poor
whites, the former living in the fertile lands and the latter
in the sand hills.

Wilson and Robertson counties in middle Tennessee and
Lowndes County in eastern, north-central Mississippi are
selected as representative of soil areas of intermediate fertility, being neither extremely fertile nor extremely poor, and
well suited for general farming as well as the growing of
money crops such as cotton and tobacco. Plantations developed in each of these counties, especially in Lowndes;
but the operating units were, as a rule, farmers rather than
planters. In the Robertson County table of twenty-six
farmers John B. Fiser, with four hundred acres under cultivation and twenty-nine slaves, is the only person who
could be classed as even a small planter. Of the thirty-three
persons listed in the Wilson County table, Antony Owens,
with eighteen slaves and five hundred acres under cultivation, and J. B. Thomas, nonslaveholder, with three hundred
acres under cultivation, are the only two who could be considered planters. Of the thirty-six persons in the Lowndes
County census table, Richard Wood is the only one who
can be ranked as a planter.

Hinds and Bolivar counties were selected as typical of
the most fertile soils in the South. Hinds is in the loess-soil
region and Bolivar is in the delta. The former, though
skirted by the Big Black and Pearl rivers along which there
was considerable swampy land, was, on the whole, high
and dry and its soil easily brought under cultivation. It is

not surprising, therefore, to find numerous small slaveholders and an occasional nonslaveholding small farmer in this county. Indeed, if one goes back to the settlement of this county he will discover that many of the slaveholders and

TABLE I

Heads of Agricultural Families
Robertson County, Tennessee, 1850

	Name	Slaves	Acres imp.	Acres unimp.	Value of farm
1	Marvel Lowe	8	200	415	$3,600
2	Caleb Keeler (millwright)	0	50	146	1,000
3	Alexander Lowe	8	150	400	4,000
4	W. E. Felts (blacksmith)	0	50	150	800
5	Whitwell Dowlin	1	50	46	400
6	Harris Dowlin	11	70	60	600
7	Joseph McCormick	0	50	50	300
8	Jno. B. Fiser	29	400	455	5,000
9	B. W. Bradley	5	250	635	3,500
10	Lucy Harris (tenant)	4	40	87	200
11	Jno. C. Balthrop	3	60	200	1,000
12	W. H. Farmer	0	60	187	650
13	James Head	0	40	58	650
14	Mathew Woodruff	1	75	125	325
15	Jas. Gower	0	20	30	150
16	Jacob Bell	6	100	800	2,000
17	Jas. O. Whited	0	60	80	420
18	Geo. Head	0	60	132	150
19	David Alley	0	40	222	200
20	Josiah Winters	0	75	107	675
21	W. H. Head	0	40	60	200
22	Jas. J. Wilson	12	100	163	1,000
23	Jas. Elliott	4	35	15	200
24	Thos. B. Williams	6	60	140	600
25	Geo. W. Farmer	0	30	79	500
26	M. W. Winters (tenant)	0	77	135	700

TABLE II

HEADS OF AGRICULTURAL FAMILIES
Wilson County, Tennessee, 1860

	NAME	Slaves	Acres imp.	Acres unimp.	Value of farm
1	Sumner Hamilton	4	75	9	$2,000
2	Allen Wilson	0	175	30	2,500
3	S. F. Anderson	7	125	150	2,800
4	Noel Keyton	0	100	10	2,000
5	Thomas Keyton	0	120	80	4,000
6	Josiah Davis	0	180	100	7,000
7	Chistifer Cobb	0	50	80	1,500
8	Sarah Hatley	0	20		400
9	Antony Owens	18	500	200	25,000
10	William E. Lacks	8	175	180	8,400
11	M. Lacks (renter)	0	15	5	300
12	W. Lacks (renter)	0	30	10	600
13	Chistifer Owens	2	100	50	3,000
14	Mary Owens	0	125	100	5,675
15	W. D. Jennings	3	120	82	6,000
16	James Bryant	0	150	175	7,000
17	Mary Bryant	0	40	20	1,200
18	John H. Byrn	5	200	200	8,000
19	John Owen	0	75	30	2,000
20	J. W. Williams	0	25	15	800
21	John Sneed	4	100	93	4,825
22	S. N. Thomas	1	100	137	5,925
23	L. V. Cannada	0	40	78	2,300
24	G. L. Smith	0	40	20	1,200
25	William Jewell	0	75	25	2,000
26	J. B. Thomas	0	300	233	10,660
27	Thomas Barkley	0	75	50	2,600
28	H. N. Thomas	0	60	70	4,500
29	Henry Darity	3	100	140	4,800
30	Hanthis Baxter	0	35	30	1,950
31	John G. Thomas	2	100	92	5,760
32	John C. Byrn	0	75	30	3,000
33	Sterling Sugs	0	50	50	1,500

TABLE III

HEADS OF AGRICULTURAL FAMILIES
Lowndes County, Mississippi, 1860

	NAME	Slaves	Acres imp.	Acres unimp.	Value of farm
1	James Wood	4	100	60	$1,600
2	John M. Basmore	1	60	140	1,000
3	James Wood	1	100	220	1,500
4	Joseph Morris	0	14	26	200
5	Robert Miller	0	12	78	400
6	W. F. Malloy	0	20	220	1,000
7	J. M. Dotson	0	60	100	800
8	R. Worthington	0	50	70	600
9	J. W. Gosa (guardian)	5	80	80	1,500
10	John Morris	10	100	100	2,000
11	Henry Wills	1	80	80	1,600
12	J. W. Lysles	0	60	200	2,000
13	Thomas Smith	9	100	500	4,000
14	Charles Revels	0	55	65	600
15	James Smith	0	40	270	1,200
16	Joseph Slown	0	40	80	500
17	Everard Downey	8	100	320	3,000
18	Jemison Loftis	1	80	120	600
19	William Hudson	0	30	90	600
20	J. C. Lawrence	2	40	50	300
21	W. L. Betts	1	22	51	1,000
22	C. H. Lance	0	50	30	400
23	W. E. Verner	16	200	280	2,000
24	J. W. Denton	0	40	40	800
25	John G. Gaston	0	50	150	1,000
26	F. A. McCown	0	30	90	1,000
27	E. M. Minter	0	60	140	1,000
28	Richard Wood	24	300	100	2,400
29	Ann Morris	0	36	50	800
30	Susan Minter	0	47	73	600
31	James C. Oden	3	20	60	400
32	John L. Kidd	0	45	75	1,000
33	James Eggar	0	65	95	8,000
34	Robert Stephenson	4	80	160	3,000
35	Ruffin Webb	0	50	230	3,000

TABLE IV

Heads of Agricultural Families
Hinds County, Mississippi, 1860

	Name	Slaves	Acres imp.	Acres unimp.	Value of farm
1	J. G. Lee	5	150	290	$3,520
2	A. Dulaney	4	95	65	1,600
3	J. J. Dees	6	35	85	1,200
4	W. Hand (renter)	11	220	100	4,800
5	R. Umderwood (renter)	3	75	121	2,352
6	A. C. Fletcher	10	100	132	2,480
7	R. McGowen	5	100	91	1,520
8	J. Ainsworth (renter)	23	250	150	6,000
9	J. Gallman	11	175	185	5,400
10	M. Holliday	14	200	59	2,815
11	M. Griffith	4	30	58	704
12	Z. Holliday	26	230	300	6,480
13	A. Gallman	11	160	160	3,440
14	L. Sinclair	6	150	160	3,840
15	C. B. Jones	37	250	135	7,700
16	J. T. Biggs	5	60	20	1,200
17	W. Wise	16	200	150	5,250
18	S. M. Miller	23	250	110	4,500
19	L. W. Carraway	25	500	360	11,335
20	T. G. Ford	15	265	494	11,385
21	J. W. Paterson	35	400	246	10,000
22	J. C. Sims	29	450	500	12,000
23	A. F. Granberry	35	500	660	10,000
24	J. A. Morgan	24	260	220	9,600
25	W. Biggs	18	300	200	6,000
26	W. S. Alsop	15	200	160	3,600
27	E. Coker	21	400	550	14,250
28	J. E. Moncure	66	1,200	1,000	18,900
29	C. E. Wolfe	27	220	100	3,200
30	F. A. Wolf	14	200	236	10,000
31	J. H. Miller	0	50	110	1,600
32	W. B. Smart	56	950	350	26,000
33	L. N. Wolfe	2	155	195	3,200

TABLE V

Heads of Agricultural Families
Bolivar County, Mississippi, 1860

NAME	Slaves	Acres imp.	Acres unimp.	Value of farm
1 Geo. W. Walton	26	400	560	$36,000
2 Iverson Gayden	74	410	400	32,000
3 T. B. Lenore	46	240	880	44,000
4 Chas. Clark	149	1,200	1,760	100,000
5 Jno. B. Flowers	0		960	10,000
6 T. J. Childres	14		440	4,000
7 C. G. Coffee	44	500	1,500	84,000
8 Polk and Rawls	86	1,400	800	70,000
9 Ike S. Robinson	0		2,000	20,000
10 Fielding B. Lewis	29	150	490	20,000
11 S. D. Harris	13	300	820	26,000
12 C. C. S. Farrar	86	500	143	30,000
13 G. L. and R. M. Lewis	53	425	550	50,000
14 Orrin Kingsley	40	1,000	380	20,000
15 F. A. Montgomery	0	200	600	3,200
16 Joseph Sellers	36	230	410	3,200
17 Livingston & Leddell	29	100	700	30,000
18 Dickerson Bell	55	360	1,950	65,250
19 A. and J. A. Rawls	9		308	3,000
20 James M. Owen	0	80	220	6,000
21 A. D. Luck	0	200	230	30,000
22 Wm. E. Starke	35	300	820	32,000
23 E. J. Girault	0	450	590	45,000
24 Wm. Kirk	0	60	1,040	35,000

large planters were originally nonslaveholders, in poor or moderate circumstances in the beginning, and that their wealth was developed from the richness of the soil (at the present time much depleted by erosion). Of the thirty-three men listed in the table, one had no slaves, seven held from two to five, three from six to ten, eight from eleven to sixteen, eight from twenty-three to twenty-nine, three from thirty-five to thirty-seven, and two held fifty-six and sixty-six.

Bolivar County was low and swampy, and large outlays of capital were required to bring the soil under cultivation. Swamps had to be drained, levees built, and the ground cleared of gigantic hardwood forests and jungles of cane-brakes. The result was that only those possessed of considerable wealth would undertake to open up a farm or plantation in this region. It will be observed, however, that of the twenty-four men listed, seven were nonslaveholders, three of whom may be classed as planters. Indeed, the non-slaveholder, E. J. Girault, had 450 acres under cultivation and grew 400 bales of cotton and 5,000 bushels of corn according to the census returns, while F. A. Montgomery, another nonslaveholder, with 200 acres under cultivation made 103 bales of cotton and 2,500 bushels of corn. Both grew numerous other crops and owned livestock valued at $5,000 and $3,000 respectively. These nonslaveholders, of course, probably found it less expensive—and certainly less hazardous in a malarial country—to hire slaves rather than own them. Compared to the size of plantations in the delta region today, these plantations were quite modest in acreage, and some would be classed as farms if the land under cultivation is used as an index.

From these tables it will be observed that there was very little tenancy. Most of the operators owned their land. Outside of the Carolinas and Virginia, which have not as yet been systematically examined, from 80 to 85 per cent of the agricultural population owned their land.

If one considers the landed resources that were available to the Southern people between the Revolution and the Civil War, it will become apparent why the bulk of the Southern rural population, nonslaveholder and slaveholder alike, acquired the ownership of farmsteads and plantations, and how it was that the herdsmen had such ample pasturage for their livestock. A goodly portion of the Federal public domain, which totaled 1,309,591,680 acres,[7] and over 200,000,000 acres of state lands in Virginia, the Carolinas, Georgia, and Texas had been open to Southerners during this period.[8] The opportunity of acquiring land was greater in the South than in the North. For example, in 1848, before the creation of Oregon Territory the area of the states and organized territories of the South was more than twice as great as that of the North, whereas the population of the South was scarcely half that of the North.[9] At all times during the interval between the Revolution and the Civil War the combined Federal and state public domains in the South were greater than those open to settlement in the North, and the population was increasingly less. But the Southern farmers had another great advantage over the Northerners in that the grain, livestock, and tobacco farmers of the upper South and the Southern highlands could and did move into the lower parts of the Northwest, whereas the Northern farmers could not profitably move South.

The tax lists and census reports enable us to determine with reasonable accuracy the social structure of the rural South, and they are in some degree a measure of the economic struggle of the people. They give us, however, only

[7] Benjamin H. Hibbard, *A History of the Public Land Policies* (New York, 1924), 78; Thomas C. Donaldson, *The Public Domain; Its History, with Statistics* (Washington, 1884); table on page 13.

[8] Samuel G. McLendon, *History of the Public Domain of Georgia* (Atlanta, 1924), *passim;* Roy M. Robbins, *Our Landed Heritage; the Public Domain* (Princeton, 1942), 9; Reuben McKitrick, *The Public Land System of Texas, 1823–1910* (Madison, 1918); and Aldon S. Lang, *Financial History of the Public Lands in Texas* (Waco, 1932), *passim.*

[9] See Donaldson, *Public Domain,* 28–29, for areas of states and territories.

an impersonal, external view; they furnish, let us say, a picture of the economic man, not the social, gregarious human. It is such documents as grand-jury reports, trial records, court minutes, and wills that furnish the vital spark and recreate the individual, the family, and the community. The wills especially, often so personal and intimate, go far toward supplying a substitute for the private letters and diaries which the common folk, unlike the planters, failed to preserve. The wills also reveal many family customs. A few excerpts should demonstrate the value of such documents in reconstructing the thoughts and attitudes and family relationships and customs of the Southern folk. The will of John Davidson of Dickinson County, Tennessee, nonslaveholder, substantial farmer, and owner of about three hundred acres of land, numerous horses and work stock, swine, and cattle, is given in part.

"In the name of God, Amen. I, John Davidson Sen'r being of sound mind but in a low state of health do make and publish this my last will and testament. First I desire that all my debts be paid as soon as possible out of the first money that comes into the hands of my beloved wife or my executor. Second, as to what property we have, we in the bonds of affection have labored for it lovingly. We have enjoyed it and now with a glad heart do I will and bequeath all that I die possessed of whether it be lands, crops of any kind, household and kitchen furniture or fowls of all kinds to my beloved wife during her natural life or widowhood for the support of herself and family."

Following this he makes the customary parting gifts to his adult children who seem already to have been given a portion of their inheritance. Then he selected two of his elder sons to manage the farm and care for their mother and the younger children, as was the custom. Thus, this plain

man of the Old South in simple eloquence of Biblical flavor
bade farewell to his beloved family and all his earthly pos-
sessions without a word of regret or complaint. Here was a
nonslaveholder, obviously a very literate person, who, together with his family, did not regard labor in the fields as
degrading.[10] Davidson's will also illustrates the custom
of deeding the land to the widow during her lifetime or
widowhood, and the designation of the older sons to manage the farm for her.

The will of James Davis of Harris County, Georgia, which
I quote in part, illustrates the conditional granting of land
in return for support. It is an example of the method used by
the Southern folk to provide social security.

"Whereas my said daughter Sarah Jane and her husband
James Lysle has agreed to live with and take care of me
during my natural life and also during the lifetime or
widowhood of my beloved wife Judith I therefore give and
bequeath unto my daughter Sarah Jane Lysle. . . .for her
sole and separate use during her natural life free and ex-
empt from the debts and liabilities of her present or any
future husband the following property. . . .containing one
hundred and a fourth acres more or less, and on her decease
to her children." But the ownership of the property was not
to pass to Sarah Jane, cautioned the father "unless her and
her husband shall remain with us until the time above mentioned," that is, until their deaths. If "they do not remain
till said time, the said land is to revert back to my estate." [11]

One finds in the wills many personal touches. Often the
testator had the last word in an old quarrel with his children
or his wife or sweetheart. Sometimes it would be in the
form of an invocation of the blessings of the Almighty upon

[10] Dickinson County (Tennessee) Will Book A, 140, W.P.A. Copy, 76.
[11] Harris County (Georgia) Wills, 1850–1875, February 5, 1849.

a den of iniquity; and sometimes it would be in plain, un-adorned, illiterate English. Green Sorrell of Chambers County, Alabama, disinherited what he, at least, regarded as a quarrelsome and unregenerate brood of sons and daughters by leaving most of his property to his grand-children, and ended his will on this pious note: "last and not least of all my requests—I earnestly request my family to live in peace with each other as far as possible for my sake and pray the blessings of God on them all." [12] William Burriss of Campbell County, Tennessee, had obviously been "feuding" with his wife—possibly a second or third wife, somewhat on the young and flirtatious side. After re-ferring to her as "Elizabeth Burriss" rather than "my be-loved wife" as was the usual practice, he grimly stated that the property he left for her support should be hers only "as long as she lives single and behaves herself." [13] Christine Calhoun of Tallapoosa County, Alabama, never liked sons-in-law in general and her sons-in-law in particular. Two of them she held in contempt. If they were not aware of this fact while the old lady was alive they were informed of it after she was buried and they could not talk back to her. "It must be understood," she explains in her will, "that the moneys [from the estate] will be paid each of the five [daughters] in their hands but not to any of the husbands. . . . But [above all] it is my wish and desire that no part of my estate shall go into the hands of David and William Paul as they have already proved so very sorry particularly David Paul." [14]

The will of Thomas Coy of Franklin County, Tennessee, bears the marks of tragedy. It was in the form of a personal

[12] Chambers County (Alabama) Wills, II, 1842–1855, June 27, 1842.
[13] Campbell County (Tennessee) Wills and Inventories, 1807–1841, 420–21, W.P.A. Copy, 70.
[14] Tallapoosa County (Alabama) Wills, I, 1838–1866, 21.

letter to intimate friends who had stood by Coy in need. Coy was laboring under great mental stress brought on by an unjust accusation. He had been accused of unfaithfulness by his sweetheart, Martha, and had been discarded by her. His lack of literacy, made to seem even worse by the strain under which Coy labored, did not conceal an underlying eloquence and sensitiveness. Certainly Coy had the last word with his sweetheart: "Friend Willick you and wife have bin friends to me through adversity as well as prosperity and will prove my thankfulness to you for it   it is no use to Raise my voice or to say a word in my defense   i am condemned by all for unfaithfulness of friendship there was never any one more unjustly condemned to my best friends I leave my best respects   Except the Boon I offer you   there is about Fifteen hundred Dollars   Give Ben Spyker my gun and watch   the remainder keep your self   you will pay W Pryor for washing   let Dr Borrough have my tools   make it write with him   Dock does not owe me anything   perhaps I owe him something   Keep all the rest yourself   O pardon me for this vast act   I cannot Buffet the waves any longer   God knows there is nobody tries harder to do right than I do   tell Martha I still think of her till death   Martha you judged me wrong But I forgive   you only misunderstood me   fairwell to all for I am not mad at nobody   God knows it   Missis Spyker as a last token of my friendship for you except the small sum of five hundred Dollars from your unworthy friend Coy. I should have made you a much better present   But I burnt it in a mistake a long with some letters and papers. Miss Spyker i am unjustly and ungreatfully [accused] i have not the strength of mind to [bear] it any longer. I am going to the mountains there to wander the balance of my Days. I give Ben my watch   Good Ben I bid you all goodby   I

am mad at none of you   God knows it." Poor Thomas Coy
had only a short time to wander in the mountains; indeed,
he probably leaped off one of the Cumberland mountain
tops, for his will was soon probated as a sign of his death.[15]

Ofttimes some little item in the will revealed the loving
care of the testator. James Whitehead of Harris County,
Georgia, after providing for the comfortable support of
his wife added this thoughtful sentence: "I give and bequeath to my wife Jane my horse and buggy in order that
she may go to meeting and visit in the neighborhood."
John J. Claxton of the same county, without imposing any
conditions, left his entire estate to his "dear wife" Nancy.
"My motive for giving all this," explained Claxton, "is to
prevent her from [the cares] of this world to enable her to
visit her friends and connections." [16]

[15] Franklin County (Tennessee) Will Book I–II, 238, W.P.A. Copy, 274.
[16] Harris County (Georgia), Wills and Bonds A, 1833–1849, 18, 19.

CHAPTER II

To the Promised Land:
The Migration and Settlement
of the Plain Folk

I. THE COMING OF THE HERDSMEN

THE MOTIVES for migrating from the old, well-established communities of the United States into the fresh lands of the state and Federal public domains varied with individuals. A debtor might flee into the wilderness and divest himself of his debts as a cow rids herself of the swarms of tormenting insects by dashing through a thicket of bushes; the lawbreaker might thus get beyond the reach of the sheriff; the complexities of family and marital relations could be permanently simplified, without wasting money on a lawyer and alimony, by a move of a hundred miles in a well-chosen direction; old vices and old cronies could be left behind by the morally bankrupt who wished to begin life anew; tragedy might be put out of mind in a country so new and exciting. Thus, sanctuary for all those desiring escape seemed to lie beyond the fringe of settlement. Indeed, going from the old communities into the new country was, to many a migrant, like passing through a doorway which closed behind him and through which he returned no more.

Others moved to the new country, not to seek escape but to be with their families and friends who were moving into the promised land. Love of adventure was often a powerful inducement to migrate. But the motive common to most immigrants was the desire to acquire the ownership or the free use of some portion of the public domain, which amounted to over 1,500,000,000 acres, including state lands.

In the settlement of the public domains of the South there were usually two distinct waves of settlers rather than the three generally ascribed to the Northern frontier. The first wave consisted of herdsmen, who subsisted primarily in a grazing and hunting economy; and in the second wave were the agricultural immigrants, coming to possess the land.

The herdsmen were a large and important element of the plain folk of the Old South. From the mid-eighteenth century to the Civil War they were the typical pioneers. Their abode extended from the Indian border back through the unsurveyed lands of the public domains, and even into the thinly but permanently settled agricultural communities. They fell into two classes, especially in the lower South. The first were those on the "cutting edge" of the frontier—where Indians and game were plentiful—who engaged in hunting and trapping as their principal occupation, and livestock grazing as a secondary pursuit. These people were constantly moving from place to place in search of better pastures and more game, including Indians; and they seldom built more than rude huts for their homes and not infrequently dwelt a few seasons in open-faced camps. As a consequence of their seminomadic life, they engaged in agriculture only to the extent of growing their vegetables and enough corn to furnish their bread. The next class, who were the main body of frontiersmen, occupied the zone of unsurveyed lands at a reasonably safe distance from the Indian border. They were the genuine herdsmen. Livestock grazing was their chief occupation, and hunting and trapping were secondary. They built better and more permanent cabins and many of them pre-empted a farm with the intention of acquiring title to it when the land was surveyed and put up for sale. They almost invariably cultivated considerable fields of corn, sweet potatoes, and vegetables. The inner edge of this group lived on the sparsely settled agricultural frontier where the lands had been surveyed and considerable portions sold. They usually owned land and were, more often than not, in a transitional stage from a grazing to an agricultural economy. Even after settling as farmers they often employed cowboys to manage the herds on the public domain until the frontier retreated to a distance.[1] Many frontiersmen passed through the three stages thus described, and finally settled as farmers and planters. Many others, however, grazed their cattle and hunted from one frontier to another until at last there was no frontier left except the great pine barrens and the broken and mountainous regions.

That the larger body of Southern pioneers should be primarily herdsmen in a land so long noted for its deficiency of livestock may seem odd. The explanation is, however, simple enough. The frontier ranges in the South were all that man and beast could desire. The stately trees were loaded with mast and nuts on which swine thrived and fattened as readily as on corn. The savannas and open forests, which had been kept clear of underbrush, first by the annual burnings by the Indians and later by the pioneer himself, billowed with wild oats and grasses, wild vetch,

[1] Victor Collat, *A Journey in America* [1796?] (Paris, 1826), 109–11, describes the two waves of frontiersmen.

and peavines "tall enough to reach the shoulders of a man on horseback." The valleys and swamps, covered with canebrakes so dense that they were almost impenetrable, furnished livestock a sweet winter pasturage and a protection from the cold. From colonial times to the Civil War and from the Atlantic coast to Texas, travelers and sojourners describe the country before it was despoiled by the settlers as a lush and verdant land, peculiarly fitted for grazing livestock.[2]

The Allegheny, Cumberland, and Ozark Mountains, and the broad pine belt, stretching along the coast from North Carolina to Texas and extending inland from one hundred to two hundred miles, were excellent ranges for cattle and swine as long as they were not overstocked and grazed too closely. The best pasture lands, however, were those most suited for agriculture; and although many graziers preferred the piney woods and mountains—because they were accustomed to such and because they could live here without being encroached upon by the agricultural folk—the greater portion of herdsmen in quest of fresh pastures drove their herds into those parts of the public domain which the immigrant farmers would shortly occupy. The result was that from the Atlantic frontier to the arid regions of the Southwest, and from colonial times until after the Civil

[2] Sallie W. Stockard, *The History of Guilford County, North Carolina* (Knoxville, 1902), 55, 56; Hope S. Chamberlain, *History of Wake County, North Carolina* (Raleigh, 1922), 69; Victor Davidson, *History of Wilkinson County* [Georgia] (Macon, 1930), 107–108; William P. Fleming, *Crisp County, Georgia, Historical Sketches* (Cordele, Ga., 1932), 24–25; Jethro Rumple, *A History of Rowan County, North Carolina* (Salisbury, 1881), 28–29, 54; A. J. Brown, *History of Newton County, Mississippi, from 1834 to 1894* (Jackson, 1894), 40–44; George G. Smith, *The Life and Letters of James Osgood Andrew, Bishop of the Methodist Episcopal Church South* (Nashville, 1883), 23; George E. Brewer, "History of Coosa County, Alabama" (MS. in Alabama Department of Archives and History, Montgomery), 48, 49.

War, the herdsmen were continuously crowded from the arable lands by the agricultural husbandmen. They were compelled to settle as farmers or to withdraw into the mountains, hills, and pine barrens, or to seek other frontiers.

Livestock grazing was a major occupation in the South as long as there were large bodies of public and unsettled lands available to the herdsmen. In colonial times fortunes were often made from herding livestock upon the wild lands of the proprietors and king. Energy and common sense, rather than money, were the ingredients of success in this business; and colonists soon possessed herds ranging from a few dozen to thousands of head.[3] Indeed, observes Alexander Gregg, "the number owned by a single individual were [often] very large, almost incredibly so." A considerable portion of the livestock in the colonial Carolinas and Georgia were wild swine, cattle, and horses, doubtless of Spanish origin, which had been trapped and roped by the early settlers and domesticated. Partly as a result of the presence of these wild horses, ". . . stock raising," says Gregg, "at once became a prolific source of wealth. Most of the early fortunes on the Peedee were made in this way." [4] A British official of the late colonial period has left a vivid picture of cattle grazing on the frontiers of South Carolina and Georgia. Here he observed great droves of cattle, sometimes as many as 1,500 in one herd, "under the auspices of cowpen keepers, which move (like unto the

[3] Joseph Schafer, The Social History of American Agriculture (New York, 1936), 93, 94, 95, 96; Lewis C. Gray, History of Agriculture in the Southern United States to 1860, 2 vols. (Washington, 1933), I, 148–51, 200–12; Bartholomew R. Carroll (ed.), Historical Collections of South Carolina, 2 vols. (New York, 1836), II, 129; Alexander Gregg, History of the Old Cheraws (Columbia, 1905), 109, 110; William A. Schaper, Sectionalism and Representation in South Carolina, in American Historical Association, Annual Report, 1900, I (Washington, 1901), 295, 318–19.

[4] Gregg, History of the Old Cheraws, 109.

ancient patriarch or the modern Bedowin in Arabia) from forest to forest in a measure as the grass wears out or as the planters approach them." [5] Another eighteenth-century observer was impressed with the "infinite number of all sorts of cattle" one saw in the South Carolina countryside and the wealth which was derived from grazing.[6]

Until well toward the end of the eighteenth century, the Piedmont, the Great Valley, and especially its tributary valleys and coves, were devoted primarily to grazing livestock. These herds were tended by cowboys living in temporary camps, and were driven when fat to Baltimore, New York, Philadelphia, Charleston, and Savannah, where they were slaughtered for domestic consumption and for export to the West Indies.[7]

As previously mentioned, the wild swine, cattle, and horses found in the Carolinas and Georgia during the colonial period were of Spanish origin. Later pioneers of the lower South found droves of these on the frontiers of Alabama, Florida, Mississippi, Louisiana, Arkansas, and, of course, Texas. Some of these frontier herds had their origin in the Spanish settlements of Florida and the Southwest, and others, no doubt, in the French colony of Louisiana.

There is considerable evidence that portions of this livestock were not running wild when the frontiersmen moved in, but rather that they were the property of the Indians. This was particularly the case in those regions settled after the Revolution. The numerous Scotch, English, and French traders, who had taken up their abode with the Indians

[5] Quoted in Schaper. *Sectionalism in South Carolina*, 295, and Gray, *History of Agriculture in the Southern United States*, I, 148.

[6] Carroll (ed.), *Historical Collections of South Carolina*, II, 129.

[7] Schafer, *The Social History of American Agriculture*, 95–96; Gilbert Imlay, *A Description of the Western Territory of North America*, (Dublin, 1793), 84.

during this period, seem to have domesticated large droves of cattle, horses, and swine, and their example was followed by the Indians. Albert J. Pickett, the pioneer historian of Alabama, has an account of one William Gregory who had settled among the Creek Indians before the Revolution. In 1792, says Pickett, Gregory is found near the site of Montgomery ". . . in the capacity of a stock keeper. He lived in a hut which contained his Indian family. . . . As far as the eye could see over the beautiful and gently rolling prairies his cattle and horses fed, undisturbed by man or beast. Nickolas White a thrifty merchant [Indian trader] owned the larger portion of this . . . flock." [8] The Indian agent William Hawkins took a census of livestock in the Creek towns on the lower Tallapoosa and Coosa rivers and on the Alabama River in 1799, and, besides the rather large droves of cattle, horses, and swine owned by traders and half-breeds whom Hawkins lists by name, he reported that all villages and towns had herds of these animals. Whether they were owned by the individual Indians or by the villages he does not say.[9] Travelers passing through the Creek territory observed domesticated cattle grazing in the woods. Adam Hodgson, for example, saw a herd of two thousand head of cattle belonging to a white rancher and smaller herds belonging to the Indians.[10]

These droves of livestock, both wild and domesticated, in the Indian nations were doubtless important sources from which the white frontiersman obtained many of his cattle and long-legged, razorback hogs. They explain in

[8] Albert J. Pickett Papers, Notebook 2, 1790, (MS. in Alabama Department of Archives and History, Montgomery).

[9] Peter Hamilton Papers, 1564–1839 (MS. in Alabama Department of Archives and History).

[10] Adam Hodgson, *Journey* (1823), 130 ff. (Typed copy of letter XIII in Alabama Department of Archives and History).

part the remarkable development of the grazing industry during the first part of the nineteenth century, especially after the War of 1812.

As the herdsmen were forced by the agricultural settlers —who cleared and fenced large fields and brought along their own smaller herds—to drive their livestock into the arable lands on new frontiers, in Georgia, Florida, Alabama, Mississippi, Louisiana, Arkansas, and Texas, the size and profits of the grazing business increased enormously. Contemporary travelers and writers were always impressed with the number and sizes of the herds of cattle and swine feeding upon the pasture lands of the public domain. Victor Collat in traveling through the lower reaches of the Mississippi Valley in 1796 observed that the droves of cattle "were so considerable . . . that few inhabitants are acquainted with the riches they possess." [11]

Estwick Evans while in that region in 1818 saw thousands of cattle feeding along the banks of the Mississippi River; [12] Thomas Nuttall at about the same time noted droves of livestock on the prairies of southwestern Louisiana and in the Red River district of Arkansas.[13] William Darby, who dwelt in the Southwest for a number of years and traveled extensively throughout the region in the preparation of his *Emigrant's Guide to the Western and Southwestern States,* published, in 1818, comments on the large droves of cattle along the lower Mississippi and in the western portions of Louisiana.[14] Samuel R. Brown, who published his *Western*

[11] Collat, *A Journey in America,* 176.

[12] Estwick Evans, *A Pedestrious Tour,* in Reuben G. Thwaites (ed.), *Early Western Travels,* 1748–1846, 32 vols. (Cleveland, 1904–1907), VIII, 303.

[13] Thomas Nuttall, *Journal of Travels into the Arkansas Territory,* in Thwaites (ed.), *Early Western Travels,* XIII, 311.

[14] William Darby, *The Emigrant's Guide to the Western and South-western States and Territories* (New York, 1818), 76–77.

Gazetteer or Emigrant's Directory the year before Darby published his *Guide* devotes a great deal of attention to livestock grazing in all parts of the frontier country. His description of Louisiana is illuminating. He describes the country around Madisonville as "peculiarly adapted to the rearing of hogs and cattle; for they neither require salt, nor attention in the winter; and nowhere in the United States are they raised in greater number than in the district under review." The reed cane, prairie grass, and the wire grass of the piney woods supplied pasturage the year around. Brown described the country around Natchitoches and Fort Claiborne as "yielding a rich and spontaneous pasturage to prodigious herds of cattle and droves of hogs"; and on the Opelousas prairies he saw "great herds of cattle and buffalo." [15] H. M. Brackenridge, who published his *Views of Louisiana* in 1817, speaks of "herds of cattle, of two or three hundred," grazing on the prairies and natural meadows in Louisiana.[16] Timothy Flint, the New England missionary who settled in Louisiana, said that the graziers on the Louisiana prairies sometimes possessed 15,000 head of cattle and 2,000 horses.[17]

Up the Mississippi River in Arkansas, Missouri, Kentucky, and Tennessee the reports were the same. In 1834 R. Baird expressed the opinion in his *Emigrant's and Traveller's Guide* that the Arkansas prairies "will [always] be the abodes of shepherds and herdsmen, like those of the oriental countries, from time immemorial." "The inhabitants of the settlements around the prairies," continues

[15] *The Western Gazetteer or Emigrant's Directory*, (Albany, 1817), 126, 133, 136.
[16] H. M. Brackenridge, *Views of Louisiana, containing Geographical, Statistical, and Historical Notes* (Baltimore, 1817), 198.
[17] Timothy Flint, *The History and Geography of the Mississippi Valley* (Cincinnati, 1832), 256.

Baird, "pursue agriculture to but a limited extent compared with the raising of cattle, horses, and mules. Some of these graziers have an immense number of livestock. A few years since three of these numbered 15,000 head of horned cattle and 2,000 horses and mules." Baird reported that "vast herds of cattle are raised on the western border of the state" of Missouri, and that "thousands are there slaughtered and the meat salted, and exported by way of New Orleans to the eastern states, or to the West Indies." [18] Except in the more rugged areas, especially the mountains, Kentucky and Tennessee were past the frontier stage when Baird prepared his *Guide,* and it would not be possible to differentiate between the livestock of the grazier and those of the farmer, that were fed and grazed in regular pastures and in unimproved lands of the neighborhood. But these states were probably the leading livestock growers at the time. Baird reports that the turnpike records at Cumberland Gap in 1829, though incomplete, showed that livestock valued at $2,780,000, chiefly from Kentucky, passed there on the way to Eastern markets. [19] Samuel Brown, writing several years earlier, reported widespread grazing on the open range in Kentucky. Hogs were particularly numerous. They were "raised with great ease, and in vast numbers, on the oak and chestnut lands in southern counties." [20] The Kentuckians were not content to graze their cattle on their own ranges. During the same period, Tilly Buttrick saw the cattlemen of Kentucky pasturing their herds north

[18] R. Baird, *View of the Valley of the Mississippi or the Emigrant's and Traveller's Guide to the West* (Philadelphia, 1834), 240, 261, 276. See also Benjamin Harding, *A Tour through the Western Country A.D. 1818 and 1819* (New London, 1819), 413.

[19] Baird, *View of the Valley of the Mississippi,* 194.

[20] *The Western Gazetteer or Emigrant's Directory,* 109–10.

of the Ohio,[21] and Fortescue Cuming, on a journey into Arkansas, found the Kentuckians grazing the lush pastures of the public domain in that territory.[22] As late as 1837 John M. Peck remarked that "much of the forest lands, in the Western [Mississippi] Valley produces a fine range for domestic animals and swine. Thousands are raised, and the emigrant, grows wealthy, from the bounties of nature, with but little labor." [23] In northern Florida cattle grazing was the chief occupation until late in the antebellum period.

The grazing of livestock on the arable lands of the public domain and the lives of the herdsmen followed a regular pattern from colonial days to the Civil War. A cattleman usually began as a poor young man, and if he became wealthy he settled down in some well-selected spot, usually as a planter, placing his livestock in charge of cowboys, who pastured them out past the fringe of settlement along with the herds of the graziers living upon the frontier. In his *Guide*, William Darby describes this planter-cattleman combination in southern and western Louisiana, where the planters lived in the Teche country on their plantations, and employed cowboys, for one-fifth the increase of the herd, to graze their livestock on the prairies far to the west. Many such cowboys acquired wealth, whereupon they in turn settled as planters and hired other cowboys to tend their herds on the frontier. Frequently, too, the smaller herdsmen settled as farmers on land which they had pur-

[21] Tilly Buttrick, *Voyages, Travels, and Discoveries, 1812–1819,* in Thwaites (ed.), *Early Western Travels,* VIII, 78.

[22] Fortescue Cuming, *Sketches of a Tour to the Western Country (1807–1809),* in Thwaites (ed.), *Early Western Travels,* IV, 298.

[23] John M. Peck, *A New Guide for Emigrants to the West* (Boston, 1837), 41.

chased; and they sent their livestock out on the frontier in charge of some member of the family, or allowed it to graze, along with that of neighboring farmers, on the unfenced farm and government lands of the community.[24]

By 1840 the better agricultural lands in the older states and in many parts of the newer ones had been sufficiently settled by farmers to interfere with grazing upon the open range, and the herdsmen had largely disappeared from such lands. Those who had not desired to settle as planters and farmers, but preferred their occupation and the frontier with its plentiful game, fresh cattle ranges, and scarcity of neighbors, took up their abode in the pine forests and in the mountains where other graziers had already settled because they preferred such country. Here, protected by the sterile, sandy soils of the piney woods and the rugged surface of the highlands, the herdsmen and hunters found sanctuary from the pursuing agricultural settlers. Thus it was agriculture rather than slavery that pressed these settlers into the less fertile and more rugged lands. This was an old phenomenon. From ancient times an agricultural economy has driven the livestock grazier into the deserts and the mountains, except in those states where the herdsmen control the government.[25]

The antebellum inhabitants of the pine belt and, to a lesser extent, of the mountains have been classified rather broadly as poor whites. While groups of the same type of people could be found scattered here and there in the rough, timbered areas that constituted numerous islands in

[24] Darby, *Emigrant's Guide*, 76–77. Cf. Schafer, *Social History of American Agriculture*, 93–97.

[25] M. J. Vidal de La Blache, *Principles of Human Geography* (edited by Emmanuel de Martonne; translated from the French by Millicent T. Bingham, 1926), 54, note 9, and 130–31.

the midst of the richer lands, the dwellers in the highlands and in the piney woods appeared to most of those who lived outside these regions to constitute the two chief bodies of poor whites. They lived in log cabins or hewn-log houses. Their means of support visible to the usual traveler who made hasty detours through the edges of the great woods and mountains were meager indeed. There were usually a few acres of corn, patches of sweet potatoes, cabbage, collards, peas, beans, pumpkins, and turnips, and perhaps a few rows of cotton and tobacco in a "deadening" where blackened stumps of pitch pine or hardwood stood like a ghost forest. There would be a lean milch cow, two or three scrubby horses, a few razorback hogs in a pole pen or roaming about the premises, and a pack of emaciated hounds. On the woodpile near by would be a fine, bright-bladed ax; and should the stranger peep into the cabin he would see homemade beds, tables, stools, and chairs, and the wall lined with pegs upon which to hang things. Over the mantel and, if there was more than one male member of the family, on the wall in racks made of horns or pronged branches cut from trees would be the shiny, long-barreled "rifle guns." If the visitor were to go up in the "loft" he would probably find hanging from pegs numerous steel traps waiting to be set or repaired. The men seemed shiftless; for they would sit almost motionless for hours like a lizard on a sunny log, whittling transparent shavings from a piece of pine or spruce and occasionally squirting a liberal quantity of tobacco juice into the eye of a pig or chicken that came too close. While the men were thus taking their ease, the women hoed the corn, cooked the dinner, or plied the loom, or even came out and took up the ax and cut wood with which to cook the dinner.[26]

[26] Olmsted, *A Journey in the Seaboard Slave States*, 348–51, gives a

Of course, the great error that casual travelers and later writers have made concerning the mountain and piney-wood folk of the antebellum South has been to consider them agriculturists. Had they lived upon the plains, their livestock economy would have been apparent; but because of the great forests their herds of cows and droves of hogs were seldom to be seen by anyone passing hurriedly through the country. Nor could the economic importance of their subsidiary occupation of hunting and trapping be realized except by one who tarried long and learned the ways of these taciturn folk. Another error that has helped develop the idea that the backwoodsmen and mountaineers as a class were poor whites has been the failure to regard them, during the period under consideration, in their true character as frontiersmen. Much of the mountain and pine areas was, except for the absence of the Indians, frontier country as truly as was the outer or Western frontier; indeed, these regions might be called the inner frontier. Great portions of the mountain country and the pine belt from Georgia to Texas were public domain until after the Civil War, and were sparsely settled and bountifully stocked with game.

A few systematic travelers, especially naturalists and those who became sojourners and studied the character and resources of a region and its people in the preparation of "geographies" and emigrant "guides," give a picture of the people of the pine barrens and mountains vastly different from writers such as Olmsted, Cairnes, and Daniel R. Hundley. So do the local historians, biographers, genealogists, and writers of autobiography and reminiscences (particularly lawyers, preachers, small-town newspaper

---

traditional picture of piney-woods people. See also *De Bow's Review*, XVIII (1855), 188–89.

editors, and doctors) who have lived in and near the pine belt and mountains, and who possessed intimate knowledge and understanding of the life and character of the folk in these regions. A brief excursion into the accounts of some of these observers will be useful in reaching a more authentic view of backwoods life.

Samuel Brown, in preparing his *Western Gazetteer,* revealed a clear understanding of the character of the great pine country of the South and the economy it would best sustain at the time. The pine country of Mississippi, which he estimated as comprising " . . . about half the state, will," he wrote, "probably forever remain an excellent range for hogs, cattle, and horses." The swampy portions of the country were, he observed, overgrown with jungles of reed cane which "gives milk and butter a fine flavor and uncommon richness"; and the open pine forests and savannas were carpeted with grass and buffalo clover.[27]

In 1840 John F.H. Claiborne of Natchez traveled slowly and systematically through the piney woods east of the Pearl River in Mississippi as a newspaper reporter in the company of a group of politicians on a political speaking tour. Claiborne's reports go right to the heart of the frontier economy of these people. It was quite obvious to him on his leisurely journey that the real business of the piney-wood folk was the grazing of cattle and hogs. The beauty and abundance of the range impressed him. Much of the country, he observed, "is covered exclusively with the long leaf pine; not broken, but rolling like the waves in the middle of the great ocean. The grass grows three feet high and hill and valley are studded all over with flowers of every hue. . . . Thousands of cattle are grazed here for market." "The people are for the most part pastoral, their herds fur-

[27] *The Western Gazetteer or Emigrant's Directory,* 230.

nishing their chief revenue." "These cattle are permitted to run in the range or forest, subsisting in summer on the luxuriant grass with which the teeming earth is clothed, and in winter on green rushes or reeds, a tender species of cane that grow in the brakes or thickets in every swamp, hollow and ravine." The trade in cattle, observed Claiborne, "has enriched many people." He was amazed at the ease with which fish, wild turkeys, and other edible game were procured, and at the great variety of food supplied the table on the shortest notice. Only one agricultural product seems to have connected these people in his mind with farming: the incredible quantities of sweet potatoes used at all meals and between meals. He recounted with gusto one occasion on which his kindly hostess surpassed the usual hospitality in dispensing sweet potatoes. He ate sweet potatoes with wild turkey and various other meats, had a potato pie for desert and roasted potatoes offered to him as a side dish, drank sweet-potato coffee and sweet-potato home brew, had his horse fed on sweet potatoes and sweet-potato vines, and when he retired he slept on a mattress stuffed with sweet-potato vines and dreamed that he was a sweet potato that someone was digging up.[28]

William H. Sparks, the jurist, who dwelt in the Natchez district, appears to have ridden the judicial circuit as lawyer and judge in the region described by Claiborne, where he had an opportunity of becoming closely acquainted with the piney-wood folk. Later, in writing his memoirs, he devoted considerable space to a description of these people. Those settlements east of the Pearl River, he said:

[28] John F. H. Claiborne, "A Trip through the Piney Woods," in *Mississippi Historical Society Publications* (Oxford-Jackson, 1898–1925), IX (1906), 514, 515, 516, 521, 522, 523, 530, 532–33.

". . . were constituted of a different people [from the agricultural population farther west]: most of them were from the poorer districts of Georgia and the Carolinas. True to the instincts of the people from whom they were descended, they sought as nearly as possible just such a country as that from which they came, and were really refugees from a growing civilization consequent upon a denser population and its necessities. They were not agriculturists in a proper sense of the term; true, they cultivated in some degree the soil, but it was not the prime pursuit of these people, nor was the location sought for this purpose. They desired an open, poor, pine country, which forbade a numerous population.

"Here they reared immense herds of cattle, which subsisted exclusively upon coarse grass and reeds which grew abundantly among the tall, long-leafed pine, and along the small creeks and branches numerous in this section. Through these almost interminable pine-forests the deer were ·abundant, and the canebrakes full of bears. They combined the pursuits of hunting and stock-minding, and derived support and revenue almost exclusively from these."

Sparks knew some of these people quite well and he records a significant interview with a man whose grandfather and grandmother had settled in the Mississippi backwoods —then the Indian country—a few years after the Revolutionary War. The grandfather, he told Sparks, migrated from Emanuel County, Georgia. "He carried with him a small one-horse cart pulled by an old gray mare, one feather bed, an oven, a frying-pan, two pewter dishes, six pewter plates, as many spoons, a rifle gun, and three deerhounds. He worried through the Creek Nation, extending then from the Oconee River [in Georgia] to the Tombigbee River [flowing through parts of eastern Mississippi and western Alabama].

"After four months of arduous travel he found his way to Leaf River, and there built his cabin; and with my grandmother, and my father, who was born on the trip in the heart of the Creek Nation, commenced to make a fortune. He found on a small creek of beautiful water a little bay land, and made his little field for corn and pumpkins upon that spot, all around was poor, barren woods, but he said it was a good range for stock; but he had not an ox or cow on the face of the earth. The truth is it looked like Emanuel County. The turpentine smell, the moan of the wind through the pine-trees, and nobody within fifty miles of him, was too captivating a concatenation to be resisted, and he rested here.

"About five years after he came, a man from Pearl River was driving some cattle by to Mobile, and gave my grandfather two cows to help drive his cattle. It was over one hundred miles, and you would have supposed it a dear bargain; but it turned out well, for the old man in about six weeks got back with six other head of cattle [he had obviously been engaged in a bit of cattle rustling]. From these he commenced to rear a stock which in time became large [which indeed, according to Sparks' account, developed into a sizeable fortune]." [29]

Samuel Brown described the Alabama pine country, which was being settled in 1817 by herdsmen, as "affording a fine range for cattle, hogs, and horses." [30] Timothy Flint in his *History and Geography of the Mississippi Valley* de-

---

[29] William H. Sparks, *The Memories of Fifty Years* (Philadelphia, 1870), 331–33.

[30] *The Western Gazetteer or Emigrant's Directory*, 10–17.

scribes the pine forests of Alabama as an excellent range for livestock, but not well suited for agriculture. This combination of poor soil and excellent pasturage, observes Flint, explains why many settlers deliberately moved into a country with poor soil. They "do not covet a country which admits of a dense population," he says. "They prefer those extensive pine barrens, in which there is such inexhaustible range for cattle, and which will not for a long time admit a dense population." "Many of the people about Mobile," continues Flint, "are shepherds, and have droves of cattle numbering from 500 to 1000. Swine are raised with great ease, when they can be guarded from their enemies, wolves, panthers, and alligators." The graziers tend their herds on "the small breed Indian horse, or Spanish Tackies, as they are called." These "are ugly, but handy and strong, and are better than the handsomer horse for service." The principal markets for livestock in these regions were Mobile, Blakely, and Pensacola.[31]

The local historian, F. L. Cherry, writing in 1883, described one portion of the pine belt of Alabama, extending up into Russell County, near which he lived for fifty years: "There is a section of country about a hundred square miles or more, between the Chewakla and the Uchee Creeks, which fifty years ago [1833] would not number more than a dozen families and they were mostly cow 'boys.' This section was known as 'Piney Woods' of Russell County, and as compared with the country on the creeks, was considered very poor, and profitably available only as a stock range. . . . As the land was nearly all public domain, and a market near at hand, the stock business was receiving considerable attention, and moderate fortunes soon accumulated."

[31] Flint, *History and Geography of the Mississippi Valley*, 216–19.

Cherry further observed that piney-woods people raised no corn the first few years, and "but little of anything else except stock which ran wild on the public domain." [32] In 1855 the pine lands of Alabama were still regarded as an unbroken forest affording "a fine stock range," practically undisturbed by the plowman; [33] indeed, until after the Civil War little change had occurred and cattle grazing still prevailed. [34]

As for the pine lands of Florida, which covered most of the state outside the Everglades, all were agreed that they were peculiarly fitted for a pastoral economy—an opinion borne out by the census returns, which show that Florida ranked next to Texas in per capita valuation of livestock in 1850 and that both ranked ahead of any of the other states in the Union. Flint described Florida in 1832 as "a fine grazing country" where "grass abounds in the open pine woods and savannas, and the swamps furnish inexhaustible supplies of winter range." "The rearing of cattle and horses, in times past, has been the chief employment" of the inhabitants. "They number their cattle by hundreds, and sometimes thousands." [35] Baird, writing about Florida two years later, said that "there is an almost boundless extent of range for cattle, horses, hogs, etc. in this country, and it will always be, as it is now in many places, a land of graziers, and of pastoral wealth. Many graziers and farmers can count, not only hundreds, but thousands of head of

[32] F. L. Cherry, "The History of Opelika and Her Agricultural Tributary Territory" (MS. in Alabama Department of Archives and History), 160, 163.

[33] "On the Forests and Timber of South Alabama," in *De Bow's Review,* XIX (1855), 611–13. Cf. Lewis Troost, "Mobile and Ohio Railroad," *ibid.,* III (1847), 322.

[34] Joseph Hodgson (ed.), *Alabama Manual and Statistical Register for 1869* (Montgomery, 1869), 18–19. Cf. *ibid.,* for 1868, 148–49.

[35] Flint, *History and Geography of the Mississippi Valley,* 199–200.

cattle." [36] Another observer wrote in 1850: "So numerous were the herds of cattle in Alachua . . . that from 7,000 to 10,000 could be seen grazing at once on Payne's Prairie; and there was a single grazier on the Wacasassa whose stock had increased in the course of a few years to the number of 3,000 without any other expense than that of herding them." [37]

Simon Peter Richardson, a Methodist circuit rider and presiding elder on practically every circuit and district in northern Florida and southern Georgia during the late antebellum period, has left his impressions of the piney-woods folk of Georgia and Florida. In 1843 he was given the Irwin circuit, composed almost exclusively of the piney woods of southern Georgia. Richardson in his autobiography describes the country and the people of this circuit: "[It] . . . reached from Mobly Bluff to the Okenefenokee swamp; a round of about two hundred and fifty miles, to be traveled in three weeks. The most of the people then lived by raising stock. . . . There were many good, kind families on the circuit. Everybody was hospitable in those days, whether he had much or little. I went round the circuit. The congregations were meager. All the church houses were small log cabins, and the seats were benches without backs. The people were nearly all dressed in homespun. . . . The whole country was a vast plain of long leaf pine forest. Sometimes the settlements were ten miles apart: but other parts were thickly settled." [38]

[36] Baird, *View of the Valley of the Mississippi*, 304.
[37] Quoted in Gray, *History of Agriculture in the Southern States*, II, 834. Chapter XXXV of this work gives an excellent sketch of the cattle business in the South.
[38] Simon P. Richardson, *The Lights and Shadows of Itinerant Life; An Autobiography* (Nashville, 1901), 26–27. See also Smith, *Life and Letters of James O. Andrew*, 23.

Richardson later occupied some of the richest charges in his conference, yet, of the fifty charges he had held when he wrote his autobiography, he considered the Irwin circuit of the pine barrens one of the most satisfactory of them all.[39]

William P. Fleming, basing his account in part upon the testimony of surviving pioneers, gives a vivid picture of Crisp County, Georgia, and its grazing economy. The pine lands of Crisp, he said: ". . . were by that very classification, adjudged not the best for farm purposes, and, besides, these lands were fearfully 'cumbered' with primitive forests of immense pines. Their adaptation to pasturage purposes, however, was apparent. Much of these lands, especially low lands hereabouts, grew wild oats in profusion, and the more elevated lands were heavily carpeted with wire grass, succulent and desirable to a prospective cattleman. A few older people now living are familiar with the fact that droves of cattle and sheep, numbering thousands, might be hidden from sight in wild oats when only a short distance from some one searching for them." Cattle, hog, and sheep raising, he continued, "was the principal business" until the sawmills cut the timber in the 1880's and 1890's.[40]

The importance of herding livestock in the Georgia pine belt and the almost exclusive devotion of its inhabitants to this business is shown in the census reports. In 1850, for example, the Georgia pine barrens, comprising about one fourth of the area of the state and having about one tenth of the population, produced over 400,000 head of cattle,

[39] Richardson, *Lights and Shadows of Itinerant Life*, 43.

[40] Fleming, *Crisp County Historical Sketches*, 24–25. See also Davidson, *History of Wilkinson County*, 107–108, for a similar description of the range in the piney woods of Georgia at an earlier time.

85,000 sheep, 356,000 swine, and 36,000 horses and mules.[41] This was nearly half the cattle, and about one sixth of the sheep, swine, horses, and mules of the state.

The mountains were better ranges than the pine belt, for the soil was often fertile. In fact, more cattle, swine, and sheep per capita were raised in the Appalachians, the Cumberland Plateau, and the Ozarks than in the bluegrass basins of Kentucky and Tennessee.[42] Because of the difficulty of the terrain, however, cattlemen and herdsmen were unable to utilize as great a territory as could be grazed in the pine belt. Those who were fortunate enough, however, to gain control of the entrance of a high valley with ranges practically encircling it, had a natural pasture into which they might turn their cattle without danger of their straying. In May, cattle, horses, and sheep were turned into the mountains and allowed to remain there until October. The owners would visit their herds once a week and salt them to keep them gentle and prevent them from straying too far. In the fall they would drive them to market, usually on the coast. Through Buncombe County alone, high in the mountains of western North Carolina, 150,000 hogs and thousands of cattle passed annually on their way to market.[43] Congressman T. L. Clingman of North Carolina in 1844 stated that according to turnpike records the value of livestock passing through this county annually was from two million to three million dollars.[44] Unlike the pine belt, however, there were many rich valleys in which grain farm-

[41] *Seventh Census,* Table XI, 377–84, for livestock, and Table I, 364–65, for population.

[42] Gray, *History of Agriculture in the Southern States,* II, 876, 884.

[43] John P. Arthur, *Western North Carolina; A History* (Raleigh, 1914), 285.

[44] Clingman to J. S. Skinner, in Charles Lanman, *Letters from the Alleghany Mountains,* (New York, 1848), 186; Arthur, *Western North Carolina; A History,* 285.

ers raised huge quantities of corn to sell to the cattlemen, to fatten the livestock for market or to feed them on their way to market. Frequently, there would be two thousand in one drove to be fed. There were numerous "stock stands" along the French Broad River which fed 90,000 to 100,000 hogs a month while en route to market.[45] While cattle were grazed in large numbers just as in the piney woods, hogs were more important than cattle, for the hardwood growth produced immense crops of chestnuts, acorns, walnuts, and hickory nuts, and in the rich, narrow valleys excellent corn could be grown.

Not only did the mountains of North Carolina contribute to this stream of porkers and cattle; but many also came from those of Kentucky and Tennessee. In 1849-1850 at least 81,000 head of swine were driven to the East coast from the mountains in the two latter states.[46]

Charles Lanman of New York, visiting East Tennessee in 1848 writes that: "The principal revenue of the people . . . is derived from the business of raising cattle, which is practiced to a considerable extent. The mountain ranges afford an abundance of the sweetest grazing food, and all that the farmer has to do in the autumn is to hunt up his stock, which have now become excessively fat, and drive them to the Charleston or Baltimore market."[47] The mountaineers of Virginia were likewise devoted primarily to grazing livestock. In 1823 Judge John H. Peyton, in a letter to his wife, described the economy of Pocahontas County where he spent a portion of his time. "Pocahontas County is a fine

[45] Arthur, *Western North Carolina; A History*, 285–87. See also E. Mitchell to T. L. Clingman, in Lanman, *Letters from the Alleghany Mountains*, 195.

[46] "The Hog Business in the West," in *De Bow's Review*, XVI (1854), 539–40.

[47] Lanman, *Letters from the Alleghany Mountains*, 153.

grazing country, and the support of the people is mainly derived from their flocks of cattle, horses, and sheep, which they drive over the mountains to market. There is little money among them except after these excursions, but they have little need of it—every want is supplied by the happy country they possess." [48] The Cumberland Plateau was covered with grass "where an immense pasturage is afforded to the cattle," observed the British traveler, George W. Featherstonhaugh, in 1834.[49] Even the oak barrens on the highland rim in Tennessee to the west of the plateau was devoted primarily to grazing cattle and hogs.[50]

Frederick Law Olmsted has left what may be accepted as a very good generalized picture of mountain economy in the late antebellum period. "The hills generally afford an excellent range, and the mast is usually good, much being provided by the chestnut, as well as the oak, and smaller nut-bearing trees. The soil of the hills is a rich dark vegetable deposit, and they cultivate upon very steep slopes. It is said to wash and gully but little, being very absorbtive. The valleys, and gaps across the mountain ranges, are closely settled, and all the feasible level ground that I saw in three weeks was fenced, and either under tillage or producing grass for hay. . . . Horses, mules, cattle and swine, are raised extensively, and sheep and goats in smaller numbers throughout the mountains, and afford almost the only articles of agricultural export." [51]

There are no adequate statistics for the livestock busi-

[48] John H. Peyton to his wife, in *Memoir of John Howe Peyton*, compiled by John Lewis Peyton (Staunton, Va., 1894), 50.

[49] George W. Featherstonhaugh, *Excursion through the Slave States*, 2 vols. (London, 1844), I, 185.

[50] William T. Hale, *History of De Kalb County, Tennessee* (Nashville, 1915), 49.

[51] Olmsted, *A Journey in the Back Country* (New York, 1860), 222–23.

ness prior to the census of 1840; but grazing as distinct from livestock feeding was of greater relative importance in the antebellum South than in any other part of the United States. Indeed, the South produced a larger number of mules, swine, and beef cattle in proportion to population than any section until 1860, when the sparsely settled Pacific states led in cattle raising.[52] In short, the South was a great livestock region. In the preface of the agricultural census of 1860 are the following statements that emphasize this point: "There are more than twice as many cattle, in proportion to population in the Western states, than in the Middle and New England States; and in the Southern States four times as many." "There are more cattle in proportion to population in the Pacific States than in any other section. The Southern States come next. The Western States stand third." In the 1860 census, published after the Civil War began, Kentucky and Missouri were included in the West (because they did not join the Confederacy, I suppose). If they had been included in the South, that section would have been even further ahead of the West in the per capita livestock production. This leading position was due largely to the presence of vast bodies of unimproved land, not only in the mountains and pine barrens but interspersed all through the less fertile and swampy areas of the arable lands. Table VI [53] gives the total area of each Southern state with the improved acreage for 1850 and 1860, and it can be seen at a glance that the bulk of land in the South was unimproved.

The states of Arkansas, Texas, and Florida had scarcely

[52] *Eighth Census of the United States, 1860: Agriculture* (Washington, 1864), cxii–cxiii, cxviii, cxxv–cxxvii.

[53] Donaldson, *Public Domain*, 28–29, gives areas of states. *Seventh Census,* Table LV, lxxxii–lxxxiii, and *Eighth Census, Agriculture,* Table I, vii, give amount of improved land of states in 1850 and 1860, respectively.

TABLE VI

States	Total acreage	Improved land	
		1850	1860
Arkansas	33,410,063	751,530	1,983,313
Florida	37,931,520	349,049	654,213
Texas	175,587,840	643,976	2,650,781
Kentucky	24,115,200	5,968,270	7,644,208
Tennessee	29,184,000	5,175,173	6,795,337
Missouri	41,836,931	2,938,425	6,246,871
Mississippi	30,179,840	3,444,358	5,065,755
Louisiana	26,461,440	1,590,025	2,707,108
Alabama	32,462,115	4,435,614	6,385,724
Georgia	37,120,000	6,378,479	8,062,758
South Carolina	21,760,000	4,072,031	4,572,060
North Carolina	32,450,560	5,453,975	6,517,284
Virginia	39,262,720	10,360,135	11,437,821
Maryland	7,119,360	2,797,905	3,002,257

been touched by the ax and plow before the Civil War, and only a fraction of the land, ranging from about one ninth of the total in Louisiana to nearly half in Maryland, was put to agricultural uses in the other Southern states in 1860.

A summary of livestock production for 1850 in the Southern states and in the Old Northwest, the section in the North that ranked next to the South, is presented in Table VII.[54] This will show the comparative value of the livestock production in the South, which was so largely based upon grazing the open range.

The relative importance of livestock production in the Northwest and the South in 1850 can be more easily seen from a comparison of the average per capita ownership of livestock in each state. Table VIII on page 51, computed from Table VII, gives the average ownership of each person in several states in terms of dollar evaluation.

[54] *Seventh Census*, Table LV, lxxxii–lxxxiii.

TABLE VII

POPULATION AND LIVESTOCK, 1850
The Old Northwest

State	Population	Horses Mules	Cattle	Sheep	Swine	Value of livestock
Ohio	1,757,556	466,820	1,358,947	3,942,929	1,964,770	$44,121,741
Indiana	931,392	321,898	714,666	1,122,493	2,263,776	22,478,555
Illinois	736,931	278,226	912,036	894,043	1,915,907	24,209,258
Michigan	341,591	58,576	274,449	746,435	205,847	8,008,734
Wisconsin	197,912	30,335	183,433	124,896	159,276	4,897,385

The South

State	Population	Horses Mules	Cattle	Sheep	Swine	Value of livestock
Virginia	1,421,666	293,886	1,076,269	1,310,004	1,829,843	$33,658,659
North Carolina	869,039	173,952	693,510	595,249	1,812,813	17,717,647
South Carolina	668,507	134,654	777,686	285,551	1,065,503	15,060,015
Georgia	906,185	208,710	1,097,528	560,435	2,168,617	25,728,416
Alabama	771,622	187,896	728,015	371,880	1,904,540	21,690,122
Florida	87,444	15,850	261,085	23,315	209,453	2,880,058
Mississippi	606,526	170,007	733,970	304,929	1,582,734	19,887,580
Arkansas	209,897	71,756	292,710	91,256	836,727	6,647,969
Louisiana	517,762	134,363	575,342	116,110	597,301	11,152,275
Texas	212,592	89,223	330,114	100,530	692,022	10,412,927
Missouri	682,044	266,986	791,510	762,511	1,702,625	19,887,580
Kentucky	982,405	381,291	752,502	1,102,091	2,891,163	29,661,436
Tennessee	1,002,717	345,939	750,762	811,591	3,104,800	29,978,416
Maryland	583,034	81,328	219,586	177,902	352,911	7,997,634

II. THE FARMERS POSSESS THE LAND

The second wave of settlers to come into the public domain were, as previously observed, the farmers and planters, who desired the ownership of the land rather than its free use. They cleared and fenced off large areas, turned out their own little herds of cattle and swine to graze on the unimproved public and private lands of the community and thus forced the graziers to withdraw and seek ranges

TABLE VIII

COMPARATIVE VALUATION OF LIVESTOCK, 1850

The Old Northwest		The South	
State	Per capita value of livestock	State	Per capita value of livestock
Wisconsin	$24.74	Arkansas	$31.67
Michigan	23.44	Florida	32.93
Ohio	25.67	Texas	48.98
Indiana	24.13	Kentucky	30.19
Illinois	32.85	Tennessee	29.89
		Missouri	29.15
		Mississippi	32.75
		Louisiana	21.53
		Alabama	28.10
		Georgia	28.39
		South Carolina	22.52
		North Carolina	20.38
		Virginia	23.67
		Maryland	13.72

undisturbed by the plow and ax. It was agriculture, then, and not slavery—as has been said repeatedly in the discussion of the pastoral economy of the frontier—that drove the herdsmen from frontier to frontier and finally into the pine barrens, hills, and mountains. After the Civil War this phenomenon was repeated when the farmers or nesters swarmed into the Great Plains and crowded the cattle ranchers farther into the more arid regions.

If slavery did not drive out the herdsmen from the good lands, what of the farmers, both the nonslaveholders and the small slaveholders? Were they crowded from the good lands by the planter and compelled to settle upon the inhospitable soil of the pine barrens and mountains? The answer to this is no. The plain farmers, who comprised the bulk of the Southern people, lived, as a rule, neither in the piney woods nor in the mountains, except in the valleys. They lived dispersed over all the arable regions of the South and were settled in considerable numbers on every type of soil adapted to agricultural uses except the swamp and river lands. The immigrant farmer usually avoided such regions because of the deadly malaria, and because of the great expense of clearing off the heavy timber and dense canebrakes and of constructing canals and dykes. Because of this unhealthfulness and the cost of bringing such lands under cultivation, even the richest planters usually shunned these swamps as long as other moderately rich land was available. The truth of the matter is that the plain farmers settled where they chose and stayed as long as it suited them. There were, however, several factors that determined the farmers' choice of location when they migrated to the new lands in the West.

The agricultural immigrant, far more than the herdsman, tended to seek out a country as nearly as possible like the one in which he formerly lived, in the matter of soil, rainfall, temperature, and appearance. The similarity of appearance was of great importance for both psychological and practical reasons. The fact that the emigrant shook from his feet the dust of his old community did not mean that he divested himself of the mental picture and love of the old countryside, of those rich limestone valleys, rolling hills, and sandy levels where the odor of the resinous pine scents the air and the tall trees moan in the wind, or of the rugged mountains with purple shadows and smoke hanging above the cove in the late afternoon, announcing the cheery news of supper cooking or the still making a run. A settler simply could never be entirely happy and feel at home unless he was surrounded by a landscape much like the one where he had spent his earlier years. Those accustomed to rugged country seldom debouched upon the plains, but migrated to a country where there were other hills, mountains, and valleys. The Ozarks, for example, were largely settled by pioneers from the Appalachians. Likewise, those who had inhabited level country usually avoided the hills unless they could settle in a wide valley with the hills in the distance. Others, who had lived in an open country, preferred to settle on an open prairie. Farmers accustomed to sandy loams and even poor sandy soils would not usually pre-empt or purchase a homestead in a region of stiff clay or "gumbo" soils.

Aside from sentiment that grows into acute nostalgia in strange surroundings, the agricultural migrants have scientific and practical reasons for selecting a country similar to the one from which they emigrate. The farmer who seeks a country similar in appearance, climate, and soil to the old community in which he has lived makes the basic and sound assumption that he can continue in the new country to grow the field crops, fruits, and vegetables, the tillage, habits, and marketing of which are part of his mental furniture. William H. Sparks, who himself had migrated west, remarked that the immigrants were sure to select their new home, whenever they could, "in the same parallel, and with surroundings as nearly like those they had left as possible. With the North Carolinian, good springwater, and pine-knots for his fire, were the *sine qua non*." [55] Paul Vidal de La Blache, the geographer, applies this principle to the migratory movements of the Chinese into the unsettled areas within their own country. "How," he asks, "could such individuals contrive to get along there, if unable to live in customary ways, and with customary means?" They must "find an environment similar to the one which they

[55] Sparks, *Memories of Fifty Years*, 20.

have been obliged to leave." [56] Isaiah Bowman observes that the primary function of the individuals who went out upon the American frontier to locate a fit place for settlement for themselves and their neighbors usually "consisted merely in finding soils and slopes that resembled those back at home that were known to be good." [57] The letters and diaries of pioneers abound with reports to those in the East that the soil and climate of the new country were like those back at home. As a result of such reassuring knowledge, "one great bugbear of pulling up stakes and removing to a distant home was greatly neutralized by this comfortable feeling that, however great the distance and the consequent toil, men knew toward what kind of haven they were faring and that they would meet there conditions which they had mastered before." [58]

It was soon known by the average person in the Eastern states, that, outside the highlands, the temperature, rainfall, and soil of the country lying to the west, until the Great Plains were approached, were sufficiently like those in the East to permit the continuation of the same types of agriculture. This information was derived in part from land prospectors and the emigrant guides prepared by such writers as William Darby, who made a careful study of these and related matters, but it came chiefly from the re-

[56] Vidal de La Blache, *Principles of Human Geography*, 68. Cf. Flint, *The History and Geography of the Mississippi Valley*, 217.

[57] Isaiah Bowman, *The Pioneer Fringe* (New York, 1931), 6.

[58] Archer B. Hulbert, *Soil: Its Influence on the History of the United States* (New Haven, 1930), 78. See also *ibid.*, 21–23; Albert B. Faust, "German Americans," in Francis J. Brown and Joseph S. Roucek (eds.), *Our Racial and National Minorities; Their History, Contributions, and Present Problems* (New York, 1937), 171; and Laurence M. Larson, *The Changing West and Other Essays* (Northfield, Minn., 1937), 11–12, 69–70, 71, for settlement of the Northwest by Europeans from similar regions.

ports of the herdsmen, who had raised their little patches
of corn, truck, tobacco, and cotton while hunting and grazing their livestock on the frontier. By 1860 the trend of
migration had been scientifically examined by the Census
Office on the basis of the nativity reports in the census
tables of 1850 and 1860, and the superintendent of the
census was able to state the fact that "the almost universal
law of internal migration is, that it moves west on the same
parallel of latitude. . . . Men seldom change their climate,
because to do so they must change their habits." [59]

Although the necessity of continuing to grow the usual
crops compelled the immigrant farmer to stay within certain
parallels of latitude or isothermal zones, it was not the sole
practical motive that prompted him to settle upon land
similar to that which he had cultivated in the East. Of great
importance was the need to continue to employ the methods and tools with which he was familiar. Those accustomed to the use of certain farm implements adapted to
one kind of soil had great difficulty in changing to another
type of soil, even though such a change did not entail any
change in their farm economy. This was particularly true
of those who, having cultivated sandy or loamy soils, moved
into gummy clays and lime soils. Indeed there has been
since ancient times a preference among agricultural folk
for a soil with a sand or silt content because of the greater
ease with which it can be cultivated. Vidal de La Blache
observes, for example, that the early agricultural communities of Europe were located on "the most easily cultivated"
and "not always the most fertile" soils. "Mellow friable
lands forming a sort of band from southern Russia to northern France" were the early abode of agricultural settlers.

[59] *Eighth Census, Population,* xxxv.

"Men began to seek out certain localities because they were easy to cultivate." [60] Another consideration of great importance in selecting a place of settlement was the character of drinking water to be found in the new country. Such consideration is easily overlooked by an urban people who take for granted a good water supply. The character of the water is largely determined by the character of the soil, except in the case of water from artesian wells and wells bored to a deep stratum. The best water was always to be found in a country with a rolling surface and light, sandy, poor soil. People who were accustomed to the cool limpid, freestone, soft water of the sandy hills could seldom be induced to remain long in a limestone region where the water was never clear and was hard and bitter. The women folk had their say at this point: washing and cooking in such water was too much for those accustomed to soft, freestone water.

The implication of this prejudice in favor of a country similar in climate, surface appearance, streams and springs, soil, and the natural growth of grass, timber, and wild flowers, is this: the farmers making new homes in the West were, in the majority of cases, not in search of the richest lands of the public domain, but merely the richest of the particular type of land to which they were accustomed back in the East. Perhaps in most cases they were content with land almost identical with that left behind, however poor such land had been. The only advantages that the new land would have were that it was fresh and cheaper, and the range would be better for livestock and game.

Naturally, therefore, the rural folk of the upper South dwelling in the limestone valleys and highlands, whose pattern of farm husbandry had been the growing of grain

[60] Vidal de La Blache, *Principles of Human Geography*, 62, 65.

and livestock, did not in migrating erupt into the lower South where climate and soil would force a radical change in farm economy and methods of cultivation. On the contrary, when they migrated, it was usually into the highlands, limestone basins, and valleys of Tennessee, Kentucky, Missouri, and northern Arkansas, and into the wooded lands across the Ohio River, where climate, soil, timber and the grasses indicated that the new country would be hospitable to the familiar old crops.

The authors of the emigrant guides, gazetteers, and geographies were thoroughly cognizant of the westward trend and of the principles of human geography governing it; and they counseled the prospective immigrant in accordance with these principles. Baird, in traveling over the West was struck with the manner in which that country had been colonized.

"The emigration to the Valley of the Mississippi," says Baird, "seems to have gone in columns, moving from the East almost due west, from the respective states from which they originated. From New England the emigrating column advanced through New York, peopling the middle and western parts of that state in its progress; but still continuing, it reached the northern part of Ohio, then Indiana, and finally Illinois. A part of the same column . . . is diverging into Michigan. . . . The Pennsylvania and the New Jersey column advanced within the parallels of latitude of those states in west Pennsylvania, and still continuing, advanced into the middle and southern parts of Ohio, and extended even into the middle parts of Indiana and Illinois. The Virginia column advanced first into the western part of the state and Kentucky—which was long a constituent part of it—, thence into the southern parts of Indiana and Illinois, until it had spread over almost the whole of Missouri. The North Carolina column advanced into East Tennessee, thence into West Tennessee, and also into Missouri. And the South Carolina and Georgia column has moved upon the extensive and fertile lands of Alabama [and Mississippi]. . . . In Arkansas, the emigrating columns of Kentucky and Tennessee predominate. . . .

"The above mentioned fact furnishes a better key than any other that I know of, to furnish a correct knowledge of the diversities of customs and manners which prevail in the Valley of the Mississippi. For if one knows what are the peculiarities of the several states east of the Allegheny mountains, he may expect them, with some shades of difference, occasioned by local circumstances, in the corresponding parallels in the West. Slavery keeps nearly within the same parallels. And so does every other peculiarity." [61]

William Darby, John M. Peck, S. H. Collins, Samuel Brown, and Timothy Flint, to name only a few of the better known authors of emigrant guides, give similar descriptions of the characteristics of the westward migration. They all give what has proved to be reasonably accurate advice as to the several temperature zones and the crops and fruits best suited to them.[62]

The Federal censuses of 1850 and 1860 fully sustain these observations on migration. In 1850 there were 142,102 free natives of Virginia living in the upper Southern states of Missouri, Kentucky, and Tennessee, and 155,978 living in the Old Northwest; but in the lower Southern states of Georgia, Florida, Alabama, Mississippi, Louisiana, Arkan-

[61] Baird, *View of the Valley of the Mississippi*, 100–101.
[62] Darby, *Emigrant's Guide to the Western and Southern States*, 121, 231; Peck, *A New Guide for Emigrants*, 62, 63, 108; S. H. Collins, *The Emigrant's Guide to and Description of the United States of America* (4th ed.; Hull, n.d.), 97, 98, *passim;* Flint, *The History and Geography of the Mississippi Valley, passim.*

sas, and Texas there were only 38,311 such Virginians. The Virginians had settled chiefly in the tobacco, grain, and livestock regions. Maryland exemplifies better than Virginia the zonal trend of the migration of agricultural folk. In 1850 over 30,000 free natives of that state were living in Virginia and Pennsylvania—obviously the western portions—54,310 in the Old Northwest, 12,277 in Tennessee, Kentucky, and Missouri, and only 4,722 in the seven states of the lower South mentioned above. Thus Maryland contributed little either to the upper or lower Southern states west of the mountains. North Carolina which, outside of the highlands, is essentially a state of the lower South, had 103,315 free natives living in Tennessee, Kentucky, and Missouri, 52,467 in the Old Northwest, and 107,912 in the newer states of the lower South.

The cotton farmers and planters of the lower states of the seaboard South did not settle to any great extent in the grain and livestock-growing states of the upper South. The Carolinas settled Georgia, and also, with considerable aid from Virginia, colonized Tennessee. The remainder of the states of the lower South were the children and grandchildren of the Carolinas, Georgia, and Tennessee. In 1850 there were 140,261 free native South Carolinians, 140,041 Georgians, 99,140 North Carolinians, and 79,640 Tennesseans living in the newer states of the lower South compared with about 43,000 from Virginia and Maryland. Though Tennessee and North Carolina had contributed heavily to the upper slave states and to the Old Northwest, South Carolina and Georgia had only 12,000 free natives in that region in 1850.[63]

The census of 1860 continues to show the westward trend of population in the South, the newer states such as

[63] *Seventh Census*, Table XV, xxxvi–xxxviii.

Alabama, Mississippi, Tennessee, and Kentucky contributing heavily to the states in the same zones to the west.[64]

The first agricultural settlers in the new farm lands in the
Southwest as a rule came from the Piedmont or "up
country" of the Carolinas and Georgia, where they had
already been engaged in the cultivation of cotton and where
the soil was similar in its clay and sand contents to much of
the soil of the new country. Local pioneer writers agree
that the early settlers of the Southwest—especially Alabama and Mississippi—were up-country Carolinians or
Tennesseans, many of whom had originally come from up-
country South Carolina. For example, most of the South
Carolinians who moved into Blount, Jefferson, and Pickens
counties in Alabama, were from the York, Abbeville, and
Fairfield districts,[65] very similar both in soil and in topography to the country in which they settled. More recent
studies show that in all parts of Alabama, as late as 1828,
most of those immigrants whose origin could be ascertained
came not from the Tidewater regions of the South Atlantic
states, but from the Piedmont, where they had been cultivating the short-staple cotton. They were usually farmers
and small planters with few slaves. Few of the Tidewater
planters migrated into the Southwest during this period,
probably because their heavy investments in land, the

[64] *Eighth Census, Population,* xxxiv, and 616–23. See also William O.
Lynch, "The Westward Flow of Southern Colonists before 1861," in
Journal of Southern History, IX (1943), 303–27.

[65] George Powell, "A Description of Blount County," in *Transactions
of the Alabama Historical Society, July 9th and 10th, 1855* (Tuscaloosa,
1855), 37–41; Nelson F. Smith, *History of Pickens County, Alabama*
(Carrollton, Ala., 1856), 37–49. See also A. B. McEachin, "History of
Tuscaloosa" (MS. copy in Alabama Department of Archives and History:
also published in Tuscaloosa *Times,* 1880); and Ezekiel Abner Powell,
"Fifty Years in West Alabama" (MS. copy in Alabama Department of
Archives and History; also published in Tuscaloosa *Gazette,* August 12,
1886–September 5, 1889).

stability of their principal money crops—rice, tobacco, and long-staple cotton—and their established social position tended to hold them where they were.[66] But it may well be that the climate of the Southwest, which was not hospitable to the culture of rice, tobacco, and long-staple cotton, was a decisive factor in retarding the migration from the low country.

These up-country cotton farmers and planters who settled in the newer lands selected, as has been suggested, the lighter sandy loam and sand and clay soils in preference to the stiff clays and rich black prairie lands. A. J. Brown, in his *History of Newton County, Mississippi,* observed that the early settlers in that region preferred the poorer sandy lands to the richer prairies and clay soils. "The prairies of the county," he wrote, "were very open; thousands of acres of this kind of land were entirely unobstructed by timber or undergrowth, and were very easily brought into a state of cultivation. The level, sandy and uplands were much more in demand, as the people much preferred the level uplands to the ridges or prairies." [67] Nettie Powell noted the same thing in Marion County, Georgia. "The section south of where Buena Vista now is and leading towards Draneville was known as 'turkey ridge,' and was not attractive to early settlers on account of the hard red clay soil [indicating rich soil] which was not easy to cultivate with the wooden plows that were then in use. The most of this region was left vacant until the middle thirties." [68]

The method of migration and settlement in the South, for rich and poor, was fairly uniform during the pioneer

[66] See especially Thomas P. Abernethy, *The Formative Period in Alabama, 1815–1828* (Montgomery, 1922), 25–26.

[67] Brown, *History of Newton County,* 54.

[68] Nettie Powell, *History of Marion County, Georgia* (Columbus, 1931), 21.

period. Friends and relatives living in the same or neighboring communities formed one or more parties and moved out together, and when they had reached the promised land they constituted a new community, which was called a "settle-ment"—and still is so called. Settlements were frequently miles apart, and the inhabitants of a single settlement would be more scattered than they had been in the old community in the East. After the first trek other settlers would come in smaller groups or in single families and fill in the interstices. These later comers would often be relatives or friends of these who had come first, or friends of their friends. Frequently church congregations would move in a body into the Southwest, or an entire hamlet or community would simply evacuate and march together into the "land of milk and honey." In describing the settlement of Wilkinson County, Georgia, Victor Davidson observes that "frequently large tracts were purchased and whole communities (from the older parts of the state and the Upper South) would move and settle on them. There were instances where congregations would follow their pastors here." One entire community from Virginia "came in a body from that State and purchased lands near each other." [69]

The migration of a family group from Abbeville, South Carolina, to Cherokee County in the Coosa River Valley of Alabama in 1835, has been described by one of the members of the group. "In November 1835," he says, "we bade adieu to friends and left the old homestead never to look upon it again. . . . Late in the afternoon of our first day's travel we were joined, as we rolled on, by my maternal grandparents and several other members of the family, the

[69] Davidson, *History of Wilkinson County,* 147, 162.

party thus numbering forty or fifty souls." [70] One of the most interesting group migrations into the wilderness was that of the Presbyterian congregation of Bethel Church, which came in a body from Williamsburg district of Columbia, South Carolina, and settled in Maury County, Tennessee, in 1808, where they established their church, "Zion," and the Zion community, which has remained virtually intact until this day.[71] The settlements at Watauga and in neighboring valleys, the Cumberland settlements, and those of the Kentucky bluegrass basin, such as Harrodsburg and Boonesboro, are all too well known as group undertakings to need more than mention. Such examples might be endlessly repeated. Thus the early communities of the newer states and territories were often transplanted organisms rather than synthetic bodies.

These groups did not move into the public domain in ignorance of their exact location; but rather, like the children of Israel, they sent their Calebs and Joshuas ahead to spy out the land and prepare the way. An early description of Blount County, Alabama, relates how the pioneer farmers chose their location and how they made ready for the families to settle in a new community. As they prepared to move into the wilderness, the prospective immigrants usually sent ". . . a few strong men, generally their sons, without families, deep into the then wilderness in the fall, to make corn and prepare for them. The father generally went with them and chose the place, and then went back to prepare for moving when the corn was made. A bushel of meal will suffice a man one month, and if he has no other

[70] J. D. Anthony, *Life and Times of Rev. J. D. Anthony: An Autobiography with a Few Original Sermons* (Atlanta, 1896), 14.

[71] Records of Zion Church, Maury County, Tennessee (microfilm copies in Joint University Libraries, Nashville, Tennessee).

than wild meat, he will require even less bread. In the fall season, place three or four men, one hundred miles in a wilderness, with proper tools and two horses, they will pack their bread stuff for the hundred miles—procure their meat —clear land—and produce corn sufficient to bread one hundred persons one year." [72] Blount County, which comprised much of northern and western Alabama at the time of the first settlement in 1816 and 1817, was settled in this fashion.

The same preparations are easily traced in the case of the family and neighbors of Senator Charles Tait. The Taits lived in Elbert County, Georgia, from which many of the early settlers of Alabama migrated. Charles Tait commissioned his son, Captain James A. Tait, to go into the public domain of Alabama territory to select a future home for the family. On February 2, 1817, the son, in company with his wife's brother and father, set out for Alabama territory on a journey of exploration. [73] The father and son had agreed on the type of place to select. There were certain characteristics that the place should possess, which the elder Tait later described in a letter to his son. It must unite salubrity, fertility, and navigation, and possess other advantages ". . . such as a stream near at hand for a mill and machinery—a never failing spring at the foot of a hillock, on the summit of which a mansion house can be built in due time; that it have an extensive back range where our cattle and hogs can graze and fatten without the aid of corn houses,

[72] Powell, "Description of Blount County," 42. See also, Brewer, "History of Coosa County," 48, for the example of Joel Speigner "spying out the lands for a group back in South Carolina."

[73] Elizabeth Caroline Tait to Charles Tait, February 5, 1817, Tait Papers, Family Letters I (B) (Alabama Department of Archives and History). At the time this letter was written Charles Tait was United States Senator from Georgia.

that on the right and left there is an extensive body of good land where will settle a number of good neighbors and from whom the pleasure and benefits of society will soon be realized." [74]

In December, 1817, following his journey of exploration, Captain Tait wrote his father that he would soon go to the Alabama territory, taking two or three Negroes with him, and would buy a few Negroes in Alabama, where they would make a corn crop. Later when it was safe, the family was to be brought to the new home.[75] With several Negroes—and, presumably, several of his neighbors—he proceeded to the present Wilcox County and became a squatter on the public domain, where he raised a crop of corn just as had the small farmers who came to Blount County in northern Alabama in the same year. After a year on the public domain he purchased some land at two dollars an acre; but the government held most of the land off the market, and he complained to his father that "we shall have to make another crop on the public land. The failure of the sale of all the townships advertised is a grievous and most mortifying disappointment to those generally settled on the land and to us in particular." [76]

In the meantime, the neighbors were moving into Alabama territory, many of them to become neighbors of the Taits at their new home near Fort Claiborne, where a place on the bluffs of a river was selected with the requirements that met the elder Tait's specifications. The son's letters show that the trek from Elbert County had begun even be-

[74] Charles Tait to James A. Tait, January 20, 1819, Tait Papers, Family Letters I (A).

[75] James A. Tait to Charles Tait, December 15, 1817, Tait Papers, Family Letters I (B).

[76] Id. to id., January 21, 1818, and January 17, 1819, Tait Papers, Family Letters I (B).

fore he himself had selected a plantation. "Mr. Goode and family started yesterday for the Alabama territory," he reported in November, 1817. "Gov. Bibb will start on Thursday I believe, Esquire Barnet was to have broke ground on Thursday last, his son-in-law Taliafero, follows in about three weeks, and I suppose his son Thomas in the course of the winter. Thus you see the present inhabitants are moving off." [77] Two weeks later James wrote his father, who was in Washington: "My cousin Davidson Hudson is here at our house now. He is just returned from Fort Claiborne and is determined to settle at that place or at some other town in that country; he will move out in the spring.

"The Miss Olivers are willing to go out with their sister [Mrs. Hudson] and if you are willing as their guardian and can make some suitable arrangement with regard to the disposition of their property. . . . I am determined to start before Christmas." [78] By the beginning of 1819 the migration from Elbert County, Georgia, to the neighborhood of Fort Claiborne seemed to be nearly completed. On January 20, 1819, Charles Tait wrote his son that "by this time, I hope, the last party under the direction and protection of Captain Goode have reached the Peach Tree-Bluff, in safety." [79]

The long move from the older states into the new territory was seldom the final move. Like a great drove of blackbirds lighting in a grain field, with each bird milling about, making short flights within the field in search of a more satisfactory location, the agricultural immigrant after reaching the region of his choice often moved about several times within the same general community before making a

[77] *Id.* to *id.* November 16, 1817, *ibid.*
[78] *Id.* to *id.* December 2, 1817, *ibid.*
[79] *Ibid.*, (A).

permanent settlement. The Tait papers imply that the Georgia immigrants followed this pattern more or less after reaching the Fort Claiborne community. They do not, however, supply the particulars that one would like to have. Nevertheless, occasionally the immigrant left accounts of the final phase of settlement after the frontier was reached. Such was true of the Ramsey family that migrated to southeast Mississippi, and the Robbins family that settled in Coosa County, Alabama. The records of these people are especially significant, since both families were of plain, farmer stock, which as a rule, left few personal letters and diaries.

In the winter of 1807–1808 the Ramsey family—consisting of the father, mother, two young boys, and a Negro woman—migrated from Georgia to the lands freshly ceded by the Choctaw Indians in southeast Mississippi. After a hazardous journey through the Indian country, made on horseback and on foot, the family reached Wayne County, Mississippi, in the late winter or early spring of 1808. The father immediately erected a log cabin on government land, and as soon as he had provided shelter for his family he commenced preparations for farming. He cut down the dense canebrake and fired the cane as soon as it would burn, thus killing the timber and clearing the ground. Without further preparation Ramsey planted his crop. "The planting [J. C. Ramsey, a son, later wrote] was done by making holes at proper distances, depositing the seed, covering with . . . earth taken out in making the hole. No fences nor plowing necessary, all that it needed was to keep down the mutton cane, [and] butter weed with the hoe. . . . But this preparation required time and labor, so that on the 4th day of July Father finished planting his corn and pumpkins. Such was the richness and character of this loam soil at that time that it required a short time for corn to mature; early killing frosts were also uncommon; so that although Father was late getting his in the ground, yet in gathering it in the fall, he not only made a plenty for home consumption but a surplus for market, and as to his pumpkin crop I recollect distinctly to have heard him say repeatedly that he 'could nearly walk all over his field stepping on pumpkins.' " [80]

Having little or no money, the family not only grew its own food but made its own clothing, shoes, and hats. The father bartered for a spinning wheel made by one of the neighbors, procured a pair of cotton cards, and made a loom "Georgia style." Ramsey then bargained for cotton with some of the neighbors who had been there long enough to grow a patch of cotton. He and his wife agreed to spin thread and weave cloth, with the aid of Dinah, the Negro girl, in payment for the cotton, which had to be picked from the seed by hand. Later, a hand gin, operated by some younger member of the family, was acquired.

"With these facilities, [says J. C. Ramsey] rough and unhandy as they were, Mother not only clothed the family but made surplus for market, which Father in the fall of that year [1808] carried to Mobile and sold for $2.50 per yard. Mobile was then under Spanish control and country produce or manufactured [was] very high." [81]

During the first year on the Mississippi frontier, the Ramsey family and the other settlers of the neighborhood "were often much annoyed with the Indians; although no violence was ever attempted by them." The Ramseys lived on the trail leading from the main Choctaw villages to

[80] A. C. Ramsey, Diary, 3–4 (MS. in Alabama Department of Archives and History). This manuscript is called a diary, but is really a memoir.
[81] Ibid., 4–5.

Mobile, where the Indians sold their furs, deerskins and bearskins and purchased powder, shot, and whiskey. On their way home, the Indians, who traveled in large groups, usually made it a point, continues Ramsey "to camp near the houses of the white settlers . . . bringing great loads of whiskey . . . conveyed in kegs." They would stay in the camp near the white settlers until they had consumed most or all of their supply of whiskey; and they would stage a big drunk. "Fighting, scratching and yelling was generally kept up as long as the whiskey held out." "They had system however in their drunken sprees. One would remain sober to protect and keep the drunken ones out of the fires, and prevent them from killing each other in their fights, and do police duty in general" and "to keep them from interrupting the white people especially the ladies." [82]

At the end of the year (1808) the elder Ramsey sold his squatter's rights—a cabin and some cleared land and other improvements—and moved two or three miles further down the Chickasawha River, a tributary of the Pascagoula River. "He appeared to take up the idea," observes his son, "that improving new places and selling them out to other new comers (and there were many) was better for him; more money in it; than to remain at one place and make larger improvements." By this method he hoped to "accumulate money sufficient to buy, or enter him a permanent home, when the government lands were put into the market; which he anticipated would be at no distant day, which was even so." On this new place, says the son, the father "made improvements like unto his former one, made one or two crops, and sold out again." [83] The next move was again down the Chickasawha River, across the Wayne County

[82] *Ibid.*, 6–7.
[83] *Ibid.*, 7–8.

line into Greene County and in the neighborhood of Bethel Church (Methodist), of which he had been a member since coming to Mississippi. "Here he was associated with a community of excellent citizens such as John McRae; William Martin; Norman McDuffie; Roderick McDuffie; Alex McIntosh; Daniel McIntosh; McInnis McLeod; Smith and others . . . most of whom were Scotch from North Carolina." These Scotch had built a church and, though doubtless Presbyterians, had "united with the Methodist church," probably because of their inability to obtain a Presbyterian minister. "Father McRae was a leading and zealous spirit in the church," observes the diarist, "occupying the position of class leader and with whom my father was soon associated in the same office." The Ramseys did not become squatters at this particular place, but rented river land. It was a sickly location, however, and after one year the family moved back some distance from the river.[84] The next year Ramsey sold his improvements and moved a short distance down the river where he again built a cabin, cleared land, and made a good crop. In 1815 he moved once more down the river, but was still only five miles from Bethel Church.[85]

At last the elder Ramsey had found the place that he wished to make his permanent home, and by his hard and unceasing toil had accumulated enough cash to make the purchase. When the government land in this community was put up for sale in 1816–18, Ramsey journeyed over to the land office at St. Stephens, on the Tombigbee River in Alabama, to make the purchase, only to find that "a brother in the church" was going to bid against him for the land on

[84] *Ibid.*, 10–13.
[85] *Ibid.*, 16–20.

which he had built a cabin and cleared fields. Finally he and
the "brother" agreed to divide the land, and Ramsey at
last acquired a farm. He was, however, grievously disap-
pointed both in his farm and in his neighbor and "brother
in the church," and he quickly sold his farm and purchased
land on Pearl River in Lawrence County, a distance of
about one hundred miles from his home in Greene County.
A move to this new community would end his connections
with the Bethel Church neighborhood in or near which he
had lived for ten years.[86]

But this last move was never made. Ramsey's unremitting
toil, year in and year out, in clearing and improving government lands and selling to squatters had broken his health.
He "consequently decided to move to the range and give up
trying to make a living by cultivating river lands," his son
informs us. He accordingly disposed of his land on Pearl
River and with the proceeds purchased cattle, sheep, and
swine. These together with the livestock which he already
owned gave him, as his son puts it, "a pretty good start of
stock." In the fall of 1819 he "gathered up his cattle, hogs,
and sheep and drove them to the range on the South side of
Red Creek . . . a distance of about twenty miles" from
Bethel Church. Here on government lands and in the midst
of a grazier's paradise, where the nearest two neighbors
were four and eight miles away, Ramsey "selected him
a place in the woods; a beautiful bluff on . . . Red
Creek." [87] Here he built a substantial log home and acquired title to his land as soon as it was put on the market.

Even though it was winter when the livestock were

[86] *Ibid.,* 20 ff.
[87] *Ibid.,* 36.

turned upon the range, the younger Ramsey remarks that "our stock of cattle that roamed around us looked fine and fat." "The grass [was] thick, long and tender, the ravines or branches, creek bottoms, covered with a thick cane or reed brake; no frost had fallen to kill off the luxuriant grass which then covered and carpeted the large plateaus of pine forest." Not only were cattle and sheep kept fat on the grass and cane but "the hog range here was equal to the necessities of the people, requiring no corn to prepare them for pork." Indeed "large fine fat porkers could be killed from the woods." [88]

The younger Ramsey was exultant over the new home and the pastoral life. Never had the family had such an abundance and variety of food: milk, butter, cheese, fat beef, pork from the range; and turkey, venison, bear meat, fish, and other wild game from woods and stream.

The Ramseys now followed the pattern of the herdsmen described previously. They cleared and cultivated fields large enough to supply themselves with vegetables, fruits, corn, wheat, and cotton for their clothing; but for money they depended on the sale of cattle and hogs and other products of the range and the forest. Each year they marketed, in Mobile, cattle, hogs, butter, eggs, chickens, peltries, venison hams, and wild turkeys "by which means many luxuries and necessities of life were supplied." [89] Eventually, however, when the population of the pine woods had become too dense for grazing as a major occupation, the Ramseys turned more and more to agriculture.

Soloman Robbins, who migrated to Alabama a few years

[88] *Ibid.*, 36–38.
[89] *Ibid.*, 53a.

after Ramsey settled in Mississippi, had been in Alabama during the Creek War as a private soldier, and had been entranced with the rich lands ceded by the Indians to the United States government. He returned to his home in North Carolina when the war ended, and prepared to move to the Alabama frontier. In 1816 he arrived on the Tallapoosa River, a few miles north of the future city of Montgomery. Here he opened up a farm; but the swampy river lands soon proved unhealthful and he moved to Autauga County on the Alabama River, a few miles to the southwest. He lived in this place about fifteen years and apparently accumulated considerable property, including a few slaves.

But Robbins was not content with his land, level and rich though it was. Indeed, it seems that he desired nothing so much as to get away from rich, level land and make his permanent home in the hilly country, for no sooner had the Creeks ceded the rugged lands north of Montgomery to the United States than Robbins moved in. His daughter, Mrs. Kate Grayson, described the migration and settlement of the family. After the Creek treaty of 1832, Robbins "moved with his family to Coosa County among the Creek Indians, and was the first settler to find a home in that county. As he moved from Autauga County [the adjoining county before Elmore was formed] he opened up his road as he went, with the help of the hands who assisted in driving his wagons and stock, horses, cattle, sheep, hogs, etc., of which he owned vast numbers, they cleared the road heading from Wetumpka to Nixburg—via Central Institute, which road is in use to this day. He bought a large tract of land from the Indians, paying them in silver (they would accept no other kind of money), and having the entire county to select from, of course he made a judicious selection and bought land unexcelled in fertility of soil, fine timber, most excellent range for stock, and watered by at least a dozen large, bold springs of never failing clear, cold, sparkling free stone water. Wild game was abundant, so plentiful indeed that father could go out any morning before breakfast and kill a deer or bring as many wild turkeys as he could carry. I have heard my mother say she often had as much as a large wash tub full of turkey breasts alone salted down at a time. I have often heard my father remark—even when eighty years of age—that if he knew of a country as fine as that when he went there, he would go to it even at his advanced age." [90] But Robbins made this their home and many of the descendants have remained within twenty-five miles of the original settlement through the fourth and fifth generations. The county was hilly, and the soil was of only moderate fertility as compared with that on the Tallapoosa and Alabama River bottoms where Robbins had first settled. But it was a healthful region, and its surface, soil, trees, and streams were like those of the Piedmont region of North Carolina, which doubtless explains why Robbins left the rich black belt and chose a rugged but beautiful country.

In the main outline, then, the migration and settlement of the agricultural population on the Southern frontier followed a pattern. The agricultural folk in migrating into the public domain sought a country as similar as possible to the country in which they had lived. The reasons for this were the natural love of familiar environment and the necessity of continuing the accustomed farm husbandry,

---

[90] Mrs. Kate Grayson to her nephew, W. O. Robbins of Elmore County. The original letter is enclosed in Brewer, "History of Coosa County." It was written about 1903.

which only a country similar to the old one in climate, soil, and natural growth could meet. The migrants thus found themselves moving in a westerly direction along those isothermal lines or temperature zones in which they had lived in the East. Grain and cattle farmers of the upper South remained such, and settled in the upper South to the west of the mountains and in the lower portion of the Old Northwest. Tobacco and cotton farmers did likewise and moved into the middle and lower Southern territories and states. Before migrating, one or more representatives of a group spied out the land, whereupon the group—which was frequently a congregation or neighborhood—moved out together and became neighbors in the new country. Here, in searching for a suitable place, they often moved about several times in the same community before making a permanent settlement.

This pattern of migration and settlement had a significant bearing upon the social and economic structure of the Old South and the New. The herdsmen, who withdrew to the rugged and sterile land in order that they might continue the occupation that they preferred, placed drastic limitations upon their own future economic well-being. As long as the pine belt and highlands were not overcrowded by man and beast, the range remained good and these semi-pastoral folk lived well and possessed a strong sense of security. They were certainly not poor whites as a class; but neither were many of them wealthy. Eventually, when these regions began to be crowded—and this was happening in a few places prior to the Civil War—the people would be compelled to graze fewer cattle and cultivate more and more land until they would find themselves farmers cultivating poor soil without much knowledge of agriculture.

Those agricultural immigrants who had deliberately shunned the fertile but tough clay and lime soils and had settled upon inferior sandy-loam lands placed limitations, though not as severe, upon their future economic prosperity in a way similar to the piney-wood and mountain folk. While many became well-to-do, few became rich; for the economic level of an agricultural people can rise but little above the level of the fertility of the soil. On such lands there were many large farmers and small planters with ten or fifteen slaves, but there were few if any large planters.

Those who moved into the rich lands were most fortunate; for while the majority of them were possessed of only moderate means at the time of settlement, nearly all rose in the economic scale and many who were poor in the beginning became immensely wealthy before 1860.

There were thus several regions differing greatly in fertility of soil, and consequently in wealth. Between these regions there was segregation; but within each region there was very little except in the swampy, river lands, where only the Negro, who had considerable immunity to malaria, could dwell in safety. Here large plantations were developed, through the means of slave labor, by planters usually living in a village or town in a more healthful locality. In the black belt outside of these sickly lowlands the property of the nonslaveholders, the small slaveholders, and the great planters lay more or less intermingled, and the census and tax lists show that the values of their lands and their agricultural productions per acre were about the same.

The former dependence upon large capital and slave labor to develop and maintain these large, swampy, river plantations may be better realized by viewing those areas at the present time. Many, perhaps most, such plantations have been abandoned since 1865. The ditches have long since filled with muck and trees and a dense growth of gum and cypress has brought back the primeval wilderness. Even white men of means have usually avoided such places, and there are few if any Negroes who have cared to become pioneers in clearing and ditching swamplands.

The following maps illustrate the pattern of landownership in the black belt of Alabama. They are based upon a land map of Greene County drawn to scale by V. Gayle Snedecor, the tax assessor of the county (1856).[91] A copy of the map is in the Alabama Department of Archives and History.

[91] The maps used here were prepared by Harriet C. Owsley. All the names of the landowners on the Snedecor map were checked against the census returns of 1860 and the tax books from 1854 to 1860, to identify the nonslaveholders and the slaveholders, and to determine the number held by each person. The classification of these landowners was indicated by superimposing upon photostatic copies of the Snedecor map shadings for each class.

Analysis of Map I

(on opposite page)

Map I is that of the old Knoxville precinct on the west bank of the Black Warrior River. This precinct is roughly the size of a township, which, it will be recalled, is 36 sections, or 23,040 acres. In this district the farms and plantations of the nonslaveholders and of the large and small slaveholders are thoroughly intermingled. Even on or near the river there were several small slaveholders and nonslaveholders, which, as previously explained, was unusual. This is probably due to the fact that the west bank of the Black Warrior at this point is high and not subject to frequent inundations, with the aftermath of stagnant swamp water and malarial mosquitoes.

Map I. Knoxville Precinct

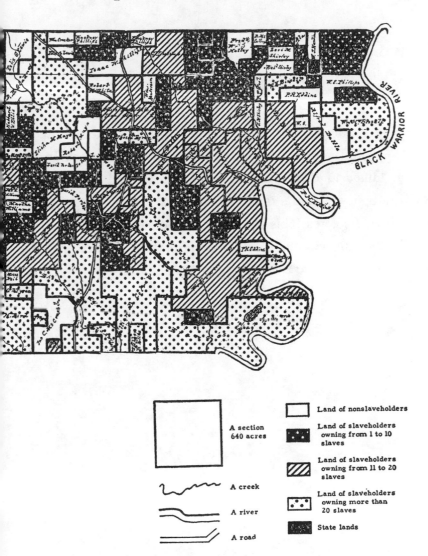

A section 640 acres

A creek

A river

A road

Land of nonslaveholders

Land of slaveholders owning from 1 to 10 slaves

Land of slaveholders owning from 11 to 20 slaves

Land of slaveholders owning more than 20 slaves

State lands

Analysis of Map II

(on opposite page)

Union precinct is represented by Map II. It lay directly behind and to the west of the Knoxville precinct. It contained in 1856, when Snedecor constructed his land map, about one and a quarter townships, that is 45 sections, or 28,800 acres. This precinct is a geological continuation of the Knoxville precinct, and the pattern of landownership was similar to that shown on Map I.

Map II. Union Precinct

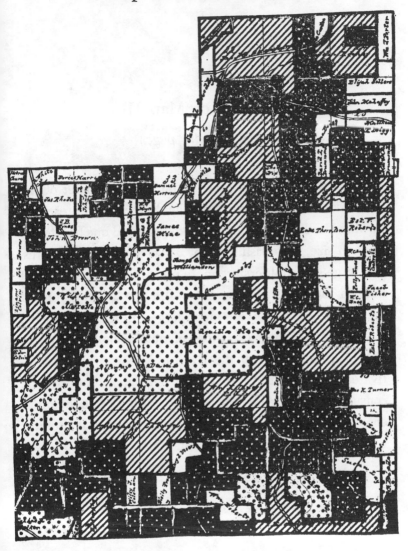

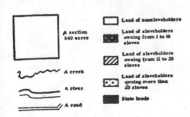

A section
640 acres

A creek

A river

A road

Land of nonslaveholders

Land of slaveholders
owning from 1 to 10
slaves

Land of slaveholders
owning from 11 to 20
slaves

Land of slaveholders
owning more than
20 slaves

State lands

Analysis of Map III

(on opposite page)

Below the Knoxville precinct on the west bank of the Black Warrior River was Springfield precinct, represented by Map III. This precinct was about one and one half townships in size, comprising about 54 sections—34,560 acres. The large slaveholders are more numerous in this precinct than in the first two examined, and the landholdings of the nonslaveholders were much larger. In fact, two of the largest plantations were those of nonslaveholders. These two plantations lay on the river and were probably cultivated by hired slave or free Negro labor. Indeed, the census returns for Greene and other black-belt counties constantly report the hiring of slaves by nonslaveholders who owned large farms and plantations.

Map III. Springfield Precinct

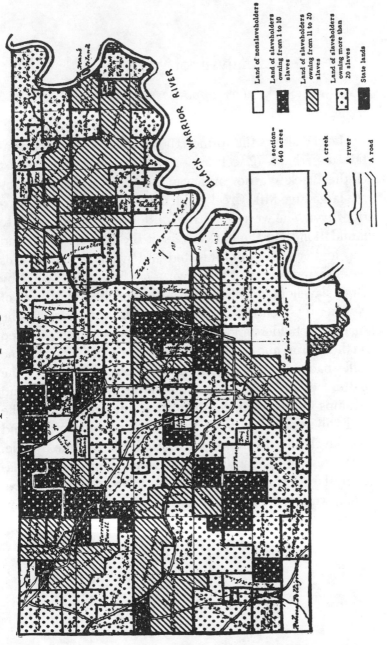

A section—
640 acres

A creek

A river

A road

Land of nonslaveholders

Land of slaveholders
owning from 1 to 10
slaves

Land of slaveholders
owning from 11 to 20
slaves

Land of slaveholders
owning more than
20 slaves

State lands

BLACK WARRIOR RIVER

Analysis of Map IV

(on opposite page)

Map IV shows the former Havana precinct, which contained, perhaps, 72 sections, or 46,080 acres. It lay just east of the Black Warrior and was bounded on the south by the large Five Mile Creek, which flows into the Black Warrior River. The western portion of this precinct is subject to inundation from the backwaters of the Black Warrior and was and is a mosquito-infested and swampy region. This western portion, near the river, was generally owned by large slaveholders, who lived in the neighboring towns of Newbern, Greensboro, and Eutaw, the county seat. The small slaveholders and nonslaveholders, who usually lived on their farms and small plantations, were to be found some miles back from the river in more healthful localities. The pattern of landownership back of the river bottoms and swamps in this precinct is similar to that in the Knoxville and Union precincts in that the lands of slaveholders and nonslaveholders were not segregated, but lay side by side. The sizes of the nonslaveholders' farms, however, are relatively large; and a few, like those in the Springfield precinct, were genuine plantations, cultivated by hired labor.

Map IV. Havana Precinct

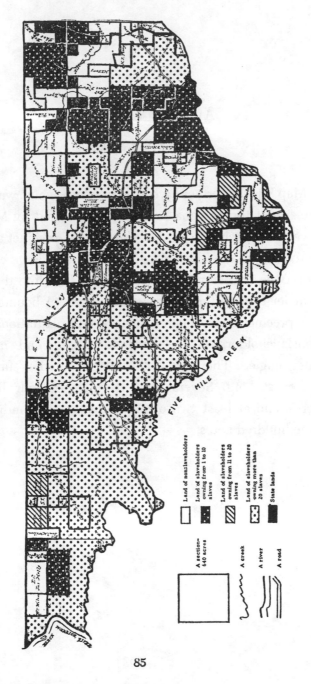

Land of nonslaveholders

Land of slaveholders
owning from 1 to 10
slaves

Land of slaveholders
owning from 11 to 20
slaves

Land of slaveholders
owning more than
20 slaves

State lands

A section—
640 acres

A creek

A river

A road

FIVE MILE CREEK

Analysis of Map V

(on opposite page)

Map V is the former Five Mile precinct, which was about the size of the Havana precinct, represented by Map IV. Five Mile precinct lay below the Havana precinct and just to the east of the Black Warrior River. Two large creeks— Five Mile Creek and Big Creek—that flow into the Black Warrior formed the northern and southern boundaries of this precinct. Here again the farms and plantations of the nonslaveholders and the slaveholders, large and small, are intermingled. The sizes of the nonslaveholders' farms are rather striking. Several owned tracts of four hundred acres, and at least two owned between six hundred and nine hundred acres.

Map V. Five Mile Precinct

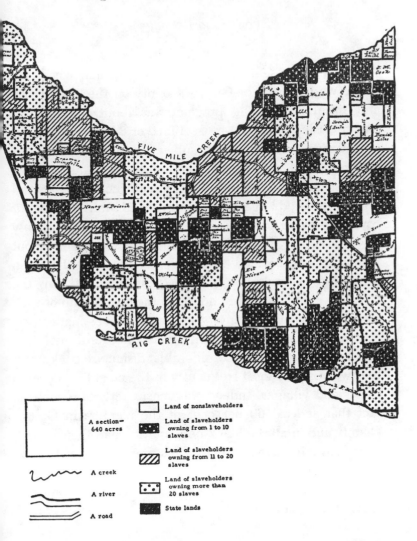

A section— 640 acres

〰〰 A creek

═══ A river

≡≡≡ A road

☐ Land of nonslaveholders

▨ Land of slaveholders owning from 1 to 10 slaves

▨ Land of slaveholders owning from 11 to 20 slaves

⋮⋮ Land of slaveholders owning more than 20 slaves

■ State lands

Analysis of Map VI

(*on opposite page*)

Map VI represents Pleasant Ridge precinct, which lay in the western part of Greene County on the Tombigbee and Sipsey rivers. This precinct was about one and one half townships in size—54 sections, or 34,560 acres. It is typical river land, swampy, subject to overflow, and formerly covered with dense canebrakes, gum, and cypress. Clearing and draining such land by constructing canals and ditches required large initial outlays of capital. White labor could not well survive in such malarial districts, and only slave labor—or that of wandering Irish ditchers about whom no one seemed to care (including the Irishmen themselves)—could be used. The result was that only the large slaveholders could undertake the opening up of such country. But these planters seldom or never made their homes here. As in other swampy areas they established their permanent residences considerable distances back from the swamps, and most frequently in the neighboring small towns and villages. Indeed the census returns reveal the fact that at least 60 per cent of the planters in Greene County and in all the black-belt counties had their permanent homes in near-by towns. This practice seems to have been common in the black belt of Mississippi, Alabama, Georgia, South Carolina, West Tennessee, and some portions of Louisiana.

Map VI. Pleasant Ridge

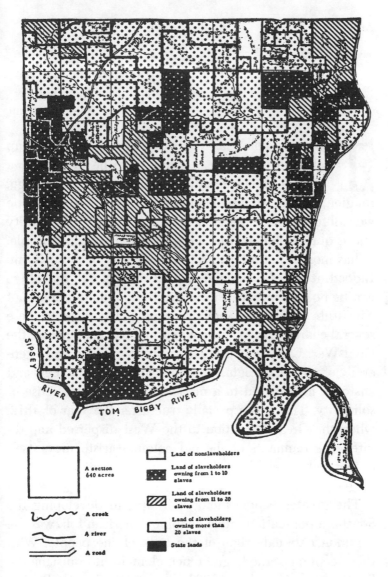

SIPSEY RIVER

TOM BIGBY RIVER

A section
640 acres

A creek

A river

A road

Land of nonslaveholders

Land of slaveholders
owning from 1 to 10
slaves

Land of slaveholders
owning from 11 to 20
slaves

Land of slaveholders
owning more than
20 slaves

State lands

Chapter III

Southern Folkways

T HE TERM "folk" has for its primary meaning a group of kindred people, forming a tribe or nation; a people bound together by ties of race, language, religion, custom, tradition, and history. Such a common tie we call folkways. A folk thus possesses a sense of solidarity and is quite different from a conglomerate mass of people. It has most if not all of the characteristics of nationalism. Indeed, it may be contended with much force that there can be no true nationalism where the population does not constitute a folk. The Southern people, according to these several characteristics, were a genuine folk long before the Civil War. Even the Southern aristocracy, who were generally of plebeian origin, were folkish in their manners and customs, and shared to a marked degree in this sense of solidarity. This was especially true after the War of 1812, when the Great Migration to the West dispersed and diluted the remnants of the old colonial aristocracy, itself descended largely from the yeomanry and middle class of England.

The greatest single factor, perhaps, in developing the Southern population into a genuine American folk was the common national origin of the bulk of the people. With the exception of the large French element in Louisiana the Southern people prior to 1860 were predominantly British, being a mixture of English and Scotch, with here and there a dash of German, French, or Irish. As a rule they were more English than Scotch in blood, but in physical appearance they probably resembled the Scotch more than they did the English or even the other Americans except in the lower part of the Midwest where so many Southern folk had settled. The English and Scotch temperaments were blended in the Southerners. They usually had the steady, easygoing nature of the English combined with an underlying Gaelic temper and humor. Fat or lean, blond or brunet, the Southern type could be discerned by travelers from abroad and from other parts of America. Appearance, the indefinable qualities of personality, and their manners and customs, particularly their distinctive speech, set them apart from the inhabitants of the other sections of the United States, and in this way strengthened their sense of kinship.

Southern folkways were in part the folkways of rural England, Scotland, and North Ireland of the sixteenth and seventeenth centuries, modified by the impact of the New World environment; and in part they were an indigenous growth of the South.

The spoken English of the South was as distinctive a characteristic of the Southern folk as corn bread, turnip greens, and sweet potatoes; and, romance to the contrary, was considered outlandish by the Northerners and the English. True, it was soft and pleasant in tone and inflection; but it had characteristics that were considered as serious defects by outsiders. Such, for example, were the drawl, the guttural "r" pronounced "ah"—and the omission of the "r" in such words as court so as to pronounce it "cote." The drawl positively irritated the English, though it usually—but not always—amused the Northerners; and the Southern use or lack of use of the "r" made the speech of the Southerners sound effeminate except to the English who treated their "r's" in a similar fashion. The employment of archaic word forms was a characteristic of the speech of the plain folk, such, for example as "yaller" for "yellow," "holped" for "helped," "fotched" for "fetched"—itself archaic in America—"ile" for "oil" and "bile" for "boil."

Though it usually has been assumed that the Southern drawl is of Negro origin, it is in reality impossible to ascertain by historical investigation the truth or falsity of this assumption. Considerable doubt, however, may be raised concerning this theory by asking the following questions. First, where did the Negro acquire his drawl, since he learned his speech from the whites? Second, from whence came the drawl of the people of the upper Great Plains and of the Blue Ridge, Smoky, and Cumberland Mountains, who have had little or no contact with the Negro? I am of the opinion that the drawl, wherever found, was originally developed by the whites in response to psychological factors, and that the Negro slave, who acquired his speech from the whites, further decreased its tempo in response to similar though not identical psychological causes. The prolongation of a word by the whites was, according to this theory, a form of politeness, and by the slave, one of deference. Here one probably finds the combination of frontier or rural influence and race temperament. To the white man on the frontier and in rural isolation, contacts with those outside the family were usually infrequent and were either highly prized or greatly dreaded—where potential enemies were involved. Under such conditions men would, so it appears, have a tendency to speak both slowly and softly to one another; for to speak quickly and in a gruff tone would sound unneighborly or unfriendly. To be unneighborly was not the desire of people of a frontier or of a rural community. To be unfriendly was dangerous, for it was regarded as a challenge to a personal encounter by people whose fighting spirit and mores did not permit the refusal of such a challenge.

The natural impulse of the Negro to be friendly and sociable and his desire to ingratiate himself with his master in order to fend off punishment or finagle the latter's best suit of broadcloth caused him to reduce the tempo of his words more than simple politeness required. Once this excessive drawl was acquired, it would be transmitted to white children who were in frequent and often constant association with Negroes.

The complex inflection, rising or falling at the sensitive points, was a characteristic of Southern speech. When combined with a soft drawl and the slight "r," it made a command sound like a request, and a request like a casual inquiry. It was, indeed, a cushion, a shock absorber for unpleasant but necessary communications; it was a balm to wounded pride and sorrow; it was also a honeyed persuader that would cause any but a Southern girl to sue a young man for breach of promise, usually—but not always —with no tangible evidence to present to court.

The speech of the plain folk and that of the more cultivated Southern people was basically the same, except, of course, the well educated would not customarily use archaic word forms. It was a speech that could not be successfully imitated. It was and is, indeed, as difficult to master as a foreign language. Few persons outside the South have ever mastered it so as to carry on a conversation without introducing false elements. For example, "you all" will be used in speaking to and of one person, whereas in true Southern English, though "you all" may be addressed to one person, its reference is always plural; it means you and your family, you and your friends, or you and your group—never just *you*. Then the drawl will be prolonged where it is not needed, and the inflection will rise or fall at the wrong spot.

The closely knit family with its ramified and widespreading kinship ties was a folk characteristic which the Southerners possessed to a degree second only to the Highland Scots of an earlier time. Though families were frequently scattered by the westward migration, they more often than not migrated and settled together. The father or the elder brother of a large family, though comfortably situated, frequently moved to the public domain or where land was cheap and plentiful to be near his sons and daughters with their husbands, or brothers and brothers-in-law with their families. Senator Charles Tait of Georgia gave expression to this pattern of behavior in a letter to his son, James, when they were preparing to migrate to Alabama: "I wish you to go where you think it will be best for you to go—where you can be more prosperous and happy. I will go where you go and stay where you stay." [1] An examination of county records, older county histories with the genealogical sketches, and, of course, the numerous genealogical works will reveal ample evidence of the cohesive quality of the family group even under the dispersive impact of the public domain.

The family was not patriarchal in the European or oriental sense, where parental authority could usually be enforced by the ability of the father to cut the son or daughter off from an inheritance. In a country where a son and even a daughter could leave the parental roof and make his or her way in the new country to the West, discipline by such

[1] February 26, 1819, Tait Papers, Family Letters I (A).

economic coercion was not feasible. We cannot, however, apply the escape-valve theory to the situation and thus come out with the conclusion that the presence of the frontier destroyed family discipline; for, as a rule, parents and grandparents exercised great influence and authority over their sons and daughters and grandsons and granddaughters, even after they were grown and married. Apparently, among the Southern folk, as among rural folk generally, age was supposed to bring wisdom rather than senility. The idea of Junior and "Honey Child" that the "old man" and the "old lady" are out of date and senile at the age of forty is decidedly an urban development.

The rural environment of the Old South where the whole family worked together, hunted together, went to church and parties together, and expected to be buried together and to come to judgment together on the Last Day, helps explain the closely knit family group. Certainly it helps explain the deference of younger persons to their parents and elders, for daily association demonstrated that "pa" knew the seasons, the habits and peculiarities of the crops; that he was a master of woodcraft, and he knew the stratagems of the chase and many other fascinating matters that only long experience and reflection could teach. "Pa" could also cut a smarter step in the reel and square dance and play the fiddle better than the boys could, and they knew it. As for "ma," it would take a lot of hard apprenticeship for the daughters to learn to cook, quilt, knit, garden, and "manage" like she could. As likely as not, too, she could dance forty different square-dance figures—and call them. In other words pa's and ma's opinions were respected because they demonstrated in their day-long work with their sons and daughters in field and house and in their play that skill and wisdom come from experience.

Religion was also a vital part of Southern folkways. Indeed, it is difficult to conceive of a genuine folk without religion. The same or similar religious beliefs and practices are an important factor in the creation of a folk, for they help bind together both the family group and the community. The Southern people, inland from the coast where the Episcopal and Catholic Churches were strong, adhered generally to the Methodist, Baptist, Presbyterian, and Church of Christ denominations with their evangelical characteristics.

The rural church, whether a small log house or a pretentious structure, was the center of a community. Here gathered rich and poor, slave and master, to hear the uncompromising champion of righteousness proclaim a gospel of eternal reward for the faithful, and for the wicked, one of eternal punishment varying from Milton's outer darkness to lakes of molten lead. To those believing but sinful souls who still had a large acreage to be sown to wild oats, such sermons were too horrible to contemplate; and they did not contemplate them. Such sinners usually stopped short of the church door and spent their time outside. They were the young bucks whom the county grand jury sometimes indicted for disturbing public worship by discharging firearms, profane swearing, and fighting near the church ground. To the saints and to those who had placed their feet upon the path of righteousness—though they might occasionally take a little detour—it was a joyous religion proclaiming a loving and forgiving God, a God who watched over the lives of his poor, earthly creatures with such care that He marked the sparrow's fall. Their happiness not infrequently moved them to loud amens and occasional loud exclamations of joy.

The church house, though reverently called the "House

of God," was also a social center, where friends and neighbors met. Many would gather on the church grounds long before services began and many would linger after the preacher had finished. The older men, singly or in small groups, would visit the graveyard. After that they discussed politics, the crops, the prospects for rain if the weather was dry, and their hopes for dry weather if it was rainy; and they laid plans for corn shuckings, logrollings, house-raisings, and other co-operative enterprises that usually combined business and pleasure. Nor was any occasion permitted to come to an end without tall tales and spicy anecdotes going their rounds. The older women, breaking quietly into little groups, would visit the churchyard, where each, perhaps, had laid away one or more children and other close relatives; and where inevitably other children and other members of the family would be buried. The churchyard was a sacred place. But these women were not overwhelmed by death. They were borne up by their religion, which promised the resurrection of the body and which taught that to give way to unrestrained grief over the death of a loved one was to question God's wisdom and His love. This sorrowful duty being performed, they chatted about their family, their gardens, flowers, chickens, clothes, and the forthcoming wedding; and planned the dinners and quiltings that accompanied the log rolling, corn shucking, or other co-operative work their menfolk had arranged.

The young men and young ladies were, of course, more preoccupied with jollification and lovemaking. They usually paired off and strolled to the spring or well. Here they conspired to gather at some neighbor's house in the afternoon to sing, and to meet again at Wednesday-night prayer services. But while plans were made for further pleasure, the pilgrimage to the well or spring was not wasted. Perhaps some couple would become engaged; and certainly each young beau would return triumphantly bearing the spoils of conquest—a rose or a cape jessamine or a bouquet as large as his mother's feather duster pinned on his lapel.

The younger children played games, hunted snakes and lizards in the woods, boasted of the prowess of their dogs or their father's mules and horses, all of which not infrequently and most naturally ended in a fight.

When at last the crowd broke up, it was not unusual for over half the congregation to go home with the others to eat late Sunday dinner. The cakes, pies, and meats—baked ham, turkey, roast pork—were already cooked and waiting in anticipation of this, for word that they were "expected" next Sunday would already have reached the ones to be invited. Only the chicken had to be fried, the biscuits cooked, and the huge pot of coffee boiled. It was not at all against the principles of the most devout for the menfolk to go to the smokehouse and uncork the wine barrel or the brown jug, to put a razor edge on the already sharp appetite in preparation for the meal that was being laid on the table in such quantities that the legs were almost buckling under the load.

The greatest social and religious events of the year were the revivals, called "protracted meetings" when held in churches, and "camp meetings" when conducted out-of-doors at regular camp grounds. They were held in the late summer after the crops were laid by and before gathering season. The best known of the camp meetings, and one that prejudiced many good people against such, was the Kentucky Cane Ridge Revival of 1800, where 20,000 or 30,000 attended, and the mighty congregation, saints and sinners, were affected by strange religious exercises, including the holy dance, the jerks, the weird holy laugh, and mass swooning. Such a camp meeting was, however, unusual both in size and in behavior. The normal camp meeting was attended by a few hundred families at most, and was usually a very orderly and, to the participants, a very enjoyable social and religious occasion.

In Georgia, the New England schoolteacher, Emily Burke, attended such a camp meeting, of which she has left an excellent account. Though she was probably a member of the Congregational Church, which generally disapproved of revivals and especially camp meetings as encouraging indecorous emotional outbursts, she was deeply impressed by the beauty and serenity of the meeting place and by the religious services. She described the camp ground as "a beautiful square lot of forest land about one acre and a half in extent, laid out amid a native and gigantic growth of oaks." On one corner of the lot was the old church which accommodated "the usual Sabbath day congregation," and on another stood a large building called "the Tabernacle" erected for the purpose of sheltering the large assemblies of the annual camp meeting. "On every side of the square, all fronting the center," says Miss Burke, "the fathers of the principal families constituting these assemblies, have each their own family residence. These little habitations are built of logs, having a piazza in front, and their number is sufficient to enclose the entire square." For the purpose of illuminating the camp grounds each householder had "erected in front of his own house a platform about six feet from the ground and four feet square, upon which . . . [was] laid earth to the depth of about one foot for the purpose of making a foundation for a fire." At twilight, fires were lighted, which "at this elevation sent forth such a broad and brilliant sheet of light in all directions, that those who seated themselves in front of their dwellings could read with perfect ease without the aid of another light."

This camp meeting was the great social event of the year, comments Miss Burke. Everyone who could possibly do so attended—rich and poor, old and young, black and white. Everything was dated with reference to whether it happened before or after the camp meeting. Young ladies planned their clothes for months in advance, and young gentlemen certainly did not neglect this matter. When all had gathered at the camp grounds, this finery was unpacked and tidied up, and in the evenings and during the intervals between services, writes Miss Burke, these "young and joyous people, richly and gaily dressed, could be seen moving in all directions, or standing in small groups beneath the shade of some wide-spreading tree, in this little city of oaks." [2]

Miss Burke speaks with admiration of the "commanding eloquence" of the ministers who preached at this camp meeting; and she felt that "on such occasion, one would not fail of having at least, an intellectual feast if not a spiritual one." But she was most deeply stirred by the simple, informal early-morning prayer services.

"The first thing in the morning [she writes], just as the sun is rising, this sleeping congregation is aroused from its slumbers by several loud and long blasts from a hunting trumpet [horn], to attend early prayers. Consequently with a slight attention to the toilet, the members of each family are soon collected together for worship. The master of the family in which I was most hospitably entertained for sev-

[2] Emily Burke, *Reminiscences of Georgia* (Oberlin, Ohio, 1850), 238, 242.

eral days was a young man of about the age of twenty six or eight, yet he presided over one of these extensive household establishments with all that ease and dignity becoming a patriarch of three score and ten. . . . As soon as we were assembled he arose and in a sweet, clear and strong voice, sung [the song] 'A Charge to keep I have, A God to glorify. . . .' We were assembled in that part of the house called the 'dining hall,' the front of which was all open to the public view, and as all the other families were similarly situated, the songs of praise which went up from each could be distinctly heard by all the rest, as they resounded that morning through every part of the camp ground." It was an experience Miss Burke would not forget. "I never expect to enjoy another scene like this beneath the skies," she later wrote.[3]

Timothy Flint, another New Englander and a missionary to the West, like Miss Burke came to regard the revival and camp meeting as a useful and beneficial institution. He describes one of the large meetings held in Tennessee in the early part of the nineteenth century.

"The notice has been [sent out] two or three months. On the appointed day, coaches, chaises, wagons, carts, people on horseback, and multitudes travelling from a distance on foot, wagons with provisions, mattresses, tents, and arrangements for the stay of a week, are seen hurrying from every point toward the central spot. It is in the midst of a grove of those beautiful and lofty trees, natural to the valleys of Tennessee, in its deepest verdue and beside a spring branch, for the requisite supply of water."[4]

All classes are there: the ambitious and the wealthy, as-

[3] *Ibid.*, 244–45.
[4] Flint, *The History and Geography of the Mississippi Valley*, 144.

pirants for office, curiosity seekers, the young and the beautiful, children, the middle aged, and the old.[5]

"The line of tents is pitched; and the religious city grows
up in a few hours under the trees beside the stream. Lamps
are hung in lines among the branches; and the effect of
their glare upon the surrounding forest is, as magic. The
scenery of the most brilliant theatre in the world is a painting only for children, compared with it. . . . By this time
the moon . . . begins to show its disk above the dark sum-
mits of the mountains; and a few stars are seen glimmering
through the intervals of branches. The whole constitutes a
temple worthy of the grandeur of God." [6]

Such a setting stimulates the imagination and arouses
the emotions. As the time for the opening of the services
approaches and the vast audience settles into its place, it
is in a receptive, even an exalted mood. Suddenly the mur-
muring of the excited multitude ceases, and there is a
strange, momentary silence of anticipation. Then "an old
man, in a dress of quaintest simplicity, ascends a platform,
wipes the dust from his spectacles, and in a voice of sup-
pressed emotion, gives out the hymn, of which the whole
assembled multitude can recite the words. . . . We should
deem poorly of the heart, that would not thrill, as the song
is heard, like the 'sound of many waters' echoing among
the hills and mountains." [7]

The song being finished, silence again settles upon the
multitude, as the old man pauses for a moment before beginning his sermon. Then, continues Flint, "the hoary ora-
tor talks of God, of eternity, a judgment to come, and all
that is impressive beyond. He speaks of his [religious] 'ex-

[5] *Ibid.*, 145.
[6] *Ibid.*
[7] *Ibid.*

periences,' his toil and travels, his persecutions and wel-
comes, and how many he has seen in hope, in peace and
triumph, gathered to their fathers; and when he speaks of
the short space that remains to him, his only regret is, that
he can no more proclaim, in the silence of death the mercies
of his crucified savior.

"There is no need of the studied trick of oratory, to produce in such a place the deepest movements of the heart.
No wonder, as the speaker pauses to dash the gathering
moisture from his eye, that his audience are dissolved in
tears, or uttering the exclamation of penitence." [8]

But there was always, according to the view, ofttimes
exaggerated of course, of the less worldly, another camp
meeting only a few hundred yards away being conducted
by Satan himself, where, according to Miss Burke, the
schoolma'am, the "rowdy element" congregated in another
tabernacle "to drink whiskey, smoke cigars, play cards, and
steal horses." Miss Burke was convinced that " 'when the
sons of God assembled together, Satan came also.' . . .
for while the fervent and incessant prayers of the righteous
ascended on high like holy incense from within, . . . the
curses and blasphemies that were poured forth from the
throats of those who had encamped round about this place
of prayer and praise, were sufficient to induce one to conclude he must have fallen somewhere near the precincts of
the infernal regions." [9]

But Satan's hosts were not invincible; for vigorous
preachers like Peter Cartwright frequently invaded the
precincts of the devil and, with a good hefty stick to whack
young sinners over the back, put the armies of darkness to
flight. Simon Peter Richardson, the Methodist presiding

[8] *Ibid.*, 145–46.
[9] Burke, *Reminiscences of Georgia*, 240–41.

elder, scattered such an unholy band at St. Mary's, Georgia, by sheer lung power. Satan's followers were having a ball in the customhouse only sixty yards from the church and had assured the preacher that they would dance him down. The dance and music had scarcely got under way, however, when Richardson sent one of the assistant preachers to the gallery to stir up the Negroes. As Richardson puts it, they "turned them loose" and their shouting drowned the music of the dance, and the "dancers left in every direction" as if pursued. "When the meeting was over," says Richardson, "we passed the custom house, and all was dark and still." [10]

In turning now to the more earthly folkways, it should be remarked that rural Southerners did not divide their lives into well-separated compartments as do their urban and even rural descendants. They often made little distinction between work and play, for all co-operative work was accompanied by play and was almost invariably followed by a party. A few examples of this co-operative work will be described, such as house-raisings, logrollings, the burning of the woods, and corn shuckings.

When a new family moved into a community and purchased land on which there was no house, or when a home burned or a couple married, it was the custom for the neighbors to gather and build a house for the homeless family or the newly wed couple. This was not just a frontier custom, though it doubtless originated on the frontier, but a rural folkway practiced in many parts of the South as late as World War I. Nor were the houses thus co-operatively raised necessarily of logs as they had been in the frontier days. On the contrary, in a country where the vast pine forests were considered encumbrances and there were numerous small sawmills, plank houses were as often put

[10] Richardson, *Lights and Shadows of Itinerant Life*, 97, 98.

up as log. If the houses were to be built of planks, the co-operative task would consist chiefly of constructing what was called "the shell"—the framework, the flooring, roof, and weatherboarding. The shell could usually be built in one or two days; and then the family could move in. After that, individual neighbors might contribute two or three days each as the time could be spared, for putting in ceiling, windows, doors, and for the general finishing. More often than not, perhaps, the finishing process was done by the owner of the house, and might extend over a number of years. One room would be ceiled one year and another later. Frequently in the warmer parts of the South nothing but doors, window shutters, a chimney, and stove flue were added after the shell was built.

Every day we see frame houses in the various stages of construction; but few if any of us have ever seen a bona fide log house being built. There are numerous contemporary descriptions of house-raisings. I will quote from one written by a man who saw log houses raised—perhaps helped raise them—many of which are standing today. This is the account that the Reverend George Brewer gives in his unpublished History of Coosa County, Alabama. Brewer lived in and near this county from the 1830's until his death, about 1922.

"The county [he writes] settled rapidly and houses were needed. At first there were no saw mills, and for sometime but few, so that sawed lumber could not be gotten at all, or only by long and expensive hauls. The consequence was that log houses were the rule. To 1850 frame houses were scarce. . . . Houses of course varied in size from the single room log hut, to the large two storied houses made of large hewn logs with verandas or awnings. The most common, however, for the average man who looked after comfort and not too much expense, was what was called the two room or double log house, with a hall [dog run] of ten or twelve feet between. The rooms were usually from 18 to 20 feet square. The walls were made of skinned poles five or six inches through, or logs of ten or twelve inches split in two in the center. After the walls were raised the split side which was inward, was hewed comparatively smooth, and the outside likewise well skelped with the broad axe. The cracks were usually lined with long boards rived from good splitting timber, and drawn to smoothness with the drawing knife. Some times if the house was desired to be very tight the cracks were chinked on the outside with split pieces of timber, and this daubed with mortar. These houses usually had shed rooms, thus making four rooms to the house; and if more room was needed, two sheds on the front some less [in length] than the main rooms [were added] so as to have a sort of open court in front of the hallway [in which a porch was built later]. These sheds were made either of poles or boards rived in long strips. The houses were covered with two- or three-foot boards rived out of blocks of these lengths sawed from good splitting trees.

"There were generally built in the back yard, some distance from the main building, separate houses for cook and dining rooms, smoke or meat houses, store room, and dairy. Stables, cribs, and barns were made in like manner, nearby, but with less care usually to appearance.

"When the logs for a house were cut and put on the ground near where the house was to be built the neighbors were invited to come to the house raising on a specified day. They would assemble by seven or eight o'clock, and after the sills had been properly placed on their pillars of sawed lightwood blocks, or rocks, four men, skillful with

an axe, were chosen as corner men, and each took possession of a corner. If the house was double eight corner men
were required. The other men brought the logs and hoisted
them to the corner men who would proceed at once to
cutting a notch so as to fit the log below after the first had
been fitted to the sill, so as to keep the wall both perpendicu-
lar and steady. Often a good fit would be secured at the first
cutting. If not, the corner men turned the log up, and re-
moddled [sic] the notch until a fit was secured. These men
had for scaffolding on which to stand while cutting and
fitting these notches only the cracks between the logs, or
. . . [the] top of the turned up log or pole. . . . A constant
run of social chat, hunting feats, stirring incidents, interesting exploits, or political matters made the time pass pleas-
antly, and more like a good natured social gathering than
the hard work it was." [11]

The midday dinner would be a feast, for the smokehouse,
pantry, chicken yard, and garden would be called on for
their choice products. If the family did not own a good
Negro cook, one would be hired, perhaps, and in any case
the women folks of the neighborhood would co-operate in
the preparation of the meal. Usually, too, the ladies would
have a quilting while the men were raising the house. The
men sat "around a long, improvised table," says Brewer,
"made gay with the jest, the joke, or lively talk." Then the
ladies, who had waited upon the men's table, would eat
while the men rested, smoked, chewed their tobacco, and
cracked jokes. After a short rest the men resumed their
work, and "usually by night the house would be raised and
the rafters (commonly skinned poles) were properly set
upon the plates, as the flattened top log was called. Another
bountiful meal for supper was eaten, and then all would

[11] Brewer, "History of Coosa County," 189a–192.

break off for home, unless a party had been decided on in connection with the house raising, in which [case] the younger members of the families would come in and share in the social function. If the 'raising' was not completed, they would come back next day and finish up." [12]

Perhaps the next co-operative jobs would be a series of logrollings. These affairs usually took place in the late winter and early spring just before spring plowing was begun. In the South, the farmers never cleared their lands by cutting the trees down and removing them, but girdled them with an ax, which would cause them to die very quickly. A crop would then be grown in this "deadening" or "new ground" with no further clearing, for there was seldom any underbrush, because of the habit, first of the Indians and then of the farmers, of burning the woods annually. During the fall and winter the deadened trees would be set on fire and many would burn in two, where they had been girdled, and would fall; others would be weakened at this point by fire and would be blown down during the year. In the spring the farmer and his boys and two or three slaves, if he owned any, would cut the branches from the fallen trees and pile them in what was nearly always called a "bresh heap." The logs were then cut into ten- or twelve-foot lengths and the neighbors were invited to a logrolling which would usually be a few days after the invitation was sent out.

On the appointed day the neighbors would gather and proceed to the field. Here they paired off, each pair having a hand stick or hand spike between them. This hand stick, made of a hickory sapling, was about five feet long and three inches in diameter and was tapered at the ends to make it easy to grasp. It was flattened on top to prevent it

[12] *Ibid.*, 192–93.

from turning. From two to four pairs of men with hand sticks were assigned to each piece of log or "cut." The hand sticks were then thrust under the log so that it would rest on the center of the sticks, and at a signal the men stooped down and grasped the ends firmly. Then, at the signal "ready," the men in a squatting position braced themselves, keeping their bodies erect and alert; and at the next signal, such as "heave," "up," or "go," they all lifted in unison, planted their feet firmly, and then walked slowly and often in step, as if marching, to the place designated for the log heap. Here they lowered the log to the ground by squatting, but taking care to keep their backs as erect as possible. The log was then rolled from the hand sticks and the men returned for another log. These men were skilled weight lifters, for it will be observed that the log was actually raised and lowered primarily by leg power. Among these people size and heft and symmetry of muscle made no impression. A man's strength was judged by his lifting power; and ofttimes a man of 140 pounds with no bulging muscles, but with sinews like steel cables, would bring up his end of the hand stick under the "butt cut" of a huge pine, while his 200-pound partner, unable to rise, would have his knuckles buried in the ground under his end of the hand stick. Such feats were called "pulling down," and no logrolling was a success in which some champion did not thus go down.

When the log pile was waist high another would be started, and in this way hundreds of such heaps would be made in a day.

While the men were thus "toting" the logs—not rolling them except to get them off the hand sticks onto the log heap—the mothers and their daughters were cooking dinner and quilting. Ward in his *History of Coffee County, Georgia*, gives some of the chief items of one of these dinners: A sixty-gallon sugar boiler filled with rice, chicken, and fresh pork backbone—a sort of camp stew; a large pot of turnip greens and corn-meal dumplings, served with a boiled ham sliced and laid on top; crackling or shortening bread; Irish potatoes; sweet potatoes; a variety of cakes; two-story biscuits; and, of course, the huge pot of coffee, so strong that it could walk, or float an iron wedge, as these folk would have expressed it. When dinnertime came, a loud and long blast or two on a hunting horn would make the announcement; whereupon all hands would lay aside their hand sticks, dispose of their tobacco cuds, take a few gulps from the jug, and lose no time in getting to the dinner table. The logrolling was usually followed by a square dance, the music for which would be furnished by a fiddler and banjo picker who played such tunes as "One Eyed Gopher" and "Squirrel Gravey" until bribed to play some other dance tune such as the "Arkansas Traveller" and "Turkey in the Straw." [13]

After the logrollings usually came the woods burning. The woods were fired each spring when the leaves and grass had dried sufficiently to burn thoroughly. This was no cabalistic ritual, as a psychologist, employed by the Bureau of Forestry during the leaf-raking era of CWA, suggested to a faculty group at Vanderbilt. It was for the practical purposes of removing dead grass and young underbrush from the cattle range and protecting the rail fences from wildfires set in the forests by careless or mischievous persons. Burning off the woods was always an exciting affair

[13] *Ibid.*, 192–96; Warren P. Ward, *Ward's History of Coffee County, Georgia* (Atlanta, 1930), 159–61; and Timothy H. Ball, *A Glance into the Great South-East; or Clarke County, Alabama and Its Surroundings from 1540 to 1877* (Grove Hill, Ala., 1882), 187; Luke E. Tate, *History of Pickens County, Georgia* (Atlanta, 1935), 63. The older county histories usually contain descriptions of logrollings.

because of the inherently dramatic and fascinating power of fire and because of the actual hazards involved.

Neighbors agreed to fire the woods on a certain date. The first step was to clear a wide strip of leaves and brush near the rail fences, either by raking or burning with a well-controlled fire. In thus creating a firebreak by the use of fire, the men and boys (this was an occasion the boys liked almost as well as Christmas) would arm themselves with long-leaf pine brushes, with which they constantly beat down any unruly flames getting too near the fence or threatening to break loose in the woods. Sometimes, of course, a gust of wind would scatter burning leaves, and like magic a great fire would spring up and go galloping and roaring through the woods. Strategy usually rendered such wild charges harmless. A portion of the men, and probably all the boys, like a good army would rush to the flanks and rear of the forest fire and set backfires which soon met and stemmed the onslaught of the conflagration. When the firebreaks were finished the forest would then be set ablaze. After that men and boys patrolled the fences to extinguish fires set by burning leaves and sparks. Occasionally, however, fire would cunningly and quietly sneak up from an unexpected direction, on the side where there were no firebreaks, and then suddenly charge the lightwood fence, pounce upon it, and devour a hundred panels and, occasionally, a mile before it could be stopped. Sometimes houses, especially barns, were burned in this way, in which case both a house-raising and a rail splitting would be necessary.

Another interesting and exciting custom was the corn shucking. On an appointed night the neighbors gathered in the barn lot and shucked a quantity of corn, sometimes as much as one hundred bushels in an evening. There were evidently several ways of conducting a corn shucking, most of which contained some element of rivalry. Often two captains would be appointed by the host, and each would choose a team. The corn would then be divided into two piles of equal size. Then came the race, the shouting and the singing of corn songs, long ago forgotten. Soon the bottle of brandy or whiskey would be put into circulation, and the tempo of the corn shucking and of the corn songs would be increased. During the evening a few would show their liquor to some extent, though it was considered disgraceful to become intoxicated. The winning team would march around their pile of corn, carrying their captain on their shoulders, singing a corn song of triumph. Sometimes but not often, some disgruntled member of the losing team, who had had too much to drink, would send a well-aimed ear of corn at the exposed head of a member of the rival team, and a fight would promptly follow, in which most would enthusiastically participate. After the corn was shucked came the shucking supper. The following is a partial list of the dishes served at a corn shucking in Rowen County, North Carolina: loaf bread, biscuits, ham, fresh pork, chicken pie, pumpkin custard or pie, apple pie, grape pie, cakes, coffee, sweet milk, buttermilk, and preserves. One type of corn shucking was that in which the young men and girls were the chief participants. The prize went to the boy or girl who found the largest number of red or multicolored ears of corn. The lucky boy could kiss any girl he chose—which would, for policy's sake and other reasons, be the girl he brought to the party. The girl who won the prize could kiss any boy she chose or make any other demand, which had to be fulfilled, even to having some silly oaf jump into a cattle pool. This kind of corn shucking was usually a very hilarious occasion. A great deal of hard work was performed with little feeling of weariness. After the corn was shucked, the supper and dance would inevitably follow, and the party would hardly break up before dawn.

Another type of corn shucking apparently had no element of rivalry in it, but was a co-operative task lightened by corn songs and rhythmic potations of corn liquor. The Reverend George Brewer, who participated in these affairs, has left a description of such a corn shucking. The portion dealing with the corn songs is worth quoting: "There were usually two or more recognized leaders in singing the corn songs, and as they would chant or shout their couplet, all the rest would join in the chorus. There was no poetry or metre, to these songs, but there was a thrill from the melody welling up with such earnestness from the singers that it was so inspiring that the hands would fly with rapidity in tearing off the shucks, and the feet [would] kick back the shucks with equal vigor. The leader would shout:

'Pull off the shucks boys, pull off the shucks,' the crowd [would] shout out in a singing chorus:

'Round up the corn boys, round up the corn'
The leader would then chant:

'The night's getting off boys, the night's getting off'
The crowd would again sing the chorus:

'Round up the corn boys, Round up the corn.'
The leader would chant:

'Give me a dram, sir, Give me a dram.'
The chorus:

'Round up the corn boys, Round up the corn'"

"This singing," says Brewer, "could be heard on a still night 2 miles."

The Reverend further recalled that when the corn was shucked, "The leaders would pick up the owner on their shoulders and carry him several times around the house, followed closely by all the others singing some of their most stirring corn songs, and praising him in their songs. After thus carrying him around in triumph, they would enter the hallway with him on their shoulders, and seat him in a chair, and with a shuffling dance, go out into the yard. A hearty dram was then given them and they were seated to a rich supper around an improvised table. Negroes and whites enjoyed these shuckings very much . . . [and] there was the best of feeling mutually among them.[14]

The most noteworthy of all co-operative undertakings was the folk custom of taking over and working or gathering the crops of a neighbor who was handicapped by his own illness or that of a member of his family. The fields would be plowed and hoed, and, in the fall, fodder would be pulled and cotton picked or tobacco cut and stripped. The women and girls ofttimes shared equally with the men in such work. Indeed, in stripping tobacco and picking cotton, the girls often excelled the men. This relief work would be done usually by the neighbors contributing hoe hands, teams, and plow hands for a certain number of days each. Another method of extending this kind of relief was what was called "swapping work," a custom that still lingers in some communities. The number of days work contributed by each neighbor would be paid back hand for hand, team for team, and day for day at a suitable time. It is probable that most farmers preferred to repay in this fashion rather than accept as a gift the aid which they had received during their illness. It should be observed, however, that

[14] Rumple, *A History of Rowan County, North Carolina*, 172; Brewer, "History of Coosa County," 197–200; Nettie Powell, *History of Marion County, Georgia* (Columbus, Ga., 1931), 33; Tate, *History of Pickens County, Georgia*, 63–64, have accounts of corn shuckings.

"swapping work" was also a community custom practiced as a matter of economy and sociability and in no way connected with illness or hardship cases. For example when a farmer had fully hoed and plowed all his fields, and had several days of idleness in prospect, he and his sons—and his slaves if he had a few—would ofttimes go into a neighbor's fields and "catch him up with his work" as the phrase went. Later, when needed, this work would be repaid. This was putting not money, but work in the bank to be drawn on when it was required.[15]

An occasion of relaxation and pleasure, especially for the men and boys, was the trip to market. The principal market was usually a county seat, in which case the farmers would time their journey so as to be present during "Big Court"—that is, the semiannual two-weeks session of the circuit court held in the spring and fall of the year. The neighbors usually journeyed to market in convoy, for mutual aid in case of breakdowns or other road trouble and for the pleasure of companionship. They would meet at a convenient rendezvous before the cock's crow, in their huge canvas-covered Conestoga wagons, which carried heavy loads of baled cotton, tobacco, corn, or other produce, topped with cowhides, skins, and furs. They carried corn for their stock, and provisions, cooking utensils, and a good supply of blankets for themselves against the possibility of a stay of several days. They would be in no hurry to get back to their farms, for there was some business to attend to in town and the probability of fun and excitement. When night came the wagon train would stop on the roadside near a stream or spring, where the stock would be watered and fed and

[15] The writer was well acquainted with this custom and shared in its practice when a boy. According to the old people of the community it was an old, neighborly custom.

a huge camp fire of logs built. Supper would be cooked, and, after a few tall yarns were spun and jokes told at the expense of some good-natured victim, they would make beds of straw and leaves near the fire, wrap themselves in their blankets, and sleep.

In the market towns there was usually a public wagon yard where wagons and teams were kept, and where the stock was fed. In connection with the wagon yard, there was usually a large building in which the men could spread their blankets, though many preferred to sleep in their covered wagons.[16]

When the farmers marketed their cargo they purchased a few farm implements, coffee, sugar, and a supply of fine woolen and cotton cloth from which to fashion Sunday clothes—the coarser fabrics usually being made at home. This being done, they proceeded to enjoy themselves. In the evenings they gathered in groups around the fires built near their wagons, swapped stories, and traded horses and mules—no tricks being barred. Some of the wagoners were fiddlers and banjo players, and, once business was disposed of, they kept their instruments singing day and night, both from the urgings of their companions and from their own unalloyed enjoyment of playing. Then, too, there was always rivalry between players as well as the natural desire of each musician to learn some new song or musical "trick" from the other.

Inevitably the jug went the rounds, especially since hard liquor seldom cost fifty cents a gallon. This, within certain limits, which were usually observed, only produced more energetic fiddling and banjo picking, gay songs, "hoe-downs," and good-natured repartee. But when excessive

[16] See Powell, *History of Marion County, Georgia*, 19, for a description of a journey to market.

drinking occurred—and there were nearly always a few, especially among the younger men, who had set their gauges too high—some became obnoxious. There were two ways of taking care of such characters: knock them out cold with another extra-stiff drink; or just knock them out cold without an extra dram. The latter was the preferred method of dealing with a drunk, especially if it was not his first offense.

The young men ran foot races, wrestled, and boxed, and there was always a horse race. The wrestling matches between two champions or "bullies," as they were called, was always a thrilling event and frequently it became a grim affair, where no holds were barred, and a man came up with all his front teeth missing and one eye hanging out of its socket.[17]

Sometimes the contests were more deadly affairs than even the stomp and gouge fighting or wrestling. Mortal enemies would come to town hoping or expecting to encounter one another. In a fashion later emulated in the mining and cow towns of the West and stereotyped in the motion pictures, each maneuvered to obtain an advantage over the other which would enable him to kill his opponent, but which would not be so obvious as to turn public opinion against him or preclude the plea of self-defense. Such calculations were in most cases useless among a folk whose average skill in the use of firearms has probably never been

[17] Many of the county and local histories give accounts of the gathering of the country people in the county seat during "Big Court" and on other important occasions such as militia musters. See, for example, Ward, *Ward's History of Coffee County, Georgia*, 118–19; Lillie M. Grubbs, *History of Worth County, Georgia* (Macon, 1934), 39–40; Luke Ward Coverly, *History of Pike County, Mississippi 1798–1876* (Nashville, 1909), 119–20; Wellington Vandiver, "History of Talladego County" (MS. in Alabama Department of Archives and History), 8–9; Arthur, *Western North Carolina*, 284.

equalled and certainly never surpassed. Such encounters more often than not resulted in both men being shot down; and if they did not die it was not because they had not been shot in a vital spot, but because they were too tough to kill. The weapons used in such informal duels, whether the men were planters or farmers, were usually the long-barrel muskets or rifles, since men were more accustomed to these than to the flintlock or cap-and-ball pistol.

Supposing, as we have, that the farmers had brought their produce to market at the county seat during "Big Court," there was much enjoyment to be had in the court-room, watching the trials and hearing the clever and often excellent oratory of the lawyers. The judge must have had the courtroom cleared on some occasions because of ir-repressible laughter among the audience. Even the judge himself must have had trouble maintaining his dignity at such trials as that of a certain old backwoodsman in Coffee County, Georgia, brought into court on the charge of petty larceny. His brother-in-law had accused the old chap of stealing one of his shoats, and the evidence was so over-whelming that the jury fined him $100 and costs. The de-fense lawyer thereupon made such an eloquent plea for the defendent, who, he said, had no hogs of his own in the woods to kill for his hungry family, that the brother-in-law broke down and wept, paid the old thief's fine, and carried the culprit home with him.[18] Certainly there were some broad grins when the district attorney arose one day in 1841 in the circuit court and read a grand-jury indict-ment charging John Freeman and Asbery Kelly of the County of Troup and the State of Georgia with the offense of petty larceny, because said parties did purloin, make off with, abduct, "steal, take and carry . . . a certain ne-

[18] Ward, *Ward's History of Coffee County, Georgia*, 119–20.

gro woman named Dilsey aged about twenty years." [19]
When he appeared in circuit court on a November day in
1850 in Troup County and with solemnity and ponderous
gravity read an indictment charging Homer B. Weeks with
malicious mischief, for having killed "a certain hog of the
female sex commonly called a sow" [20] there must have been
guffaws and horselaughter in the rural audience.[21]

There were other group activities where fun and amusement were the principal objectives, although some economic motive was frequently involved. Years of tedious
practice were often required to attain the skill necessary
for the enjoyment of some of these activities. Such was the
fine art of hunting. In the preparation for this sport,
skill in the use of the rifle and musket, a full understanding of the habits and even the psychology of the wild creatures of the forest, and a thorough knowledge of woodcraft were essential. No man, though he could not
read his own name, who had mastered these skills was
an ignorant person. Reference was previously made to
the unexcelled skill of the Southern folk in the use
or firearms, especially the rifle. This skill, which was
exhibited so dramatically at the battle of New Orleans
and in an occasional duel, was acquired for the purpose of the chase; any other use to which it was put
was incidental and even accidental. Contemporary descriptions of this expert marksmanship abound; but there
is no better account than that of the naturalist, Philip H.

[19] Troup County [Georgia] Superior Court Records L, 102.
[20] *Ibid.*, Records N, 573.
[21] The grand-jury reports furnished a valuable insight into certain phases
of Southern life. One senses on the one hand the stern, unbending morality
of the older members of the community, and on the other the fun-loving
attitude, ranging from harmless deviltry to malicious mischief, on the part
of the young people.

Gosse, who taught school for a while in the vicinity of Selma, Alabama. I will quote him in part:

"The long rifle is familiar to every hand; skill in the use of it is the highest accomplishment which a southern gentleman glories in; even the children acquire an astonishing expertness in handling this deadly weapon. . . .

"But skill as a marksman is not estimated by quite the same standard as in the old country. Pre-eminence in any art must bear a certain relation to the average attainment; and where this is universally high, distinction can be won only by something very exalted. Hence, when the young men meet together to display their skill, curious tests are employed, which remind one of the days of old English archery, when splitting the peeled wand at a hundred paces, and such like, were the boast of the greenwood bowman. Some of these practices I had read of but here I find them in frequent use. 'Driving the nail' is one of these; a stout nail is hammered into a post about half way up to the head; the riflemen then stand at an immense distance, and fire at the nail; the object is to hit the nail so truly on the head with the ball as to drive it home. To hit it at all on one side, so as to cause it to bend or swerve, is failure; missing it altogether is out of the question.

"Another feat is 'threading the needle.' An augur-hole is pierced through the center of an upright board; the orifice is just large enough to allow the ball to pass without touching; and it is *expected* to pass without touching. A third is still more exciting—'snuffing the candle.' It is performed in the night, and the darkness of the scene adds a wildness to the amusement that greatly enhances its interest. A calm night is chosen; half-a-dozen ends of tallow candle and a box of matches are taken out into the field, whither the uproarious party of stalwart youths repair. One of them takes his station by the mark; a stick is thrust perpendicularly in the ground, on the top of which a bit of candle is fixed either in a socket, or by means of a few drops of grease. A plank is set behind the candle, to receive the balls, which are all carefully picked out after the sport is over, being much too valuable to be wasted. The marker now lights the candle, which glimmers like a feeble star, but just visible at the spot where the expectant party are standing. Each one carefully loads his rifle; some mark the barrel with a line of chalk to aid the sight in the darkness; others neglect this, and seem to know the position of the 'pea' by instinct. There is a sharp short crack, and a line of fire; a little cloud of smoke rises perpendicularly upwards; an unmerciful shout of derision hails the unlucky marksman, for the candle is still twinkling dimly and redly as before. Another confidently succeeds; the light is suddenly extinguished; his ball has cut it off just below the flame. This won't do; the test of skill is to *snuff* the candle, without putting it out.

"A third now steps up; it is my friend Jones, the overseer on the plantation where I am residing; he is a crack shot, and we all expect something superb now. The marker has replaced the lighted candle; it is allowed to burn a few minutes until the wick has become long. The dimness of the light at length announces its readiness, and the marker cries 'Fire!' A moment's breathless silence follows the flash and the report; a change was seen to pass upon the distant gleam, and the dull red light has suddenly become white and sparkling. 'Right good!' cries the marker; the ball has passed through the centre of the flame and 'snuffed the candle,' and whoops and shouts of applause ring through the field, and echo from the surrounding forest. This extraordinary feat is usually performed two or three times in every contest." [22]

Gosse tells about another common feat with the long rifle known as "barking off the squirrel." He describes how his host took him out in the yard and shot a squirrel from the top of a tall beech tree. "The ball," he says, "struck the trunk of the tree beneath the belly of the animal, driving off a piece of the bark as large as one's hand, and with it the squirrel, without a wound or a ruffled hair, but killed by the concussion." [23]

John James Audubon, the naturalist, during his sojourn in Kentucky went hunting with Daniel Boone, then an elderly man, and watched him "bark off" a pile of squirrels in a short time. Audubon likewise witnessed the same type of rifle-shooting contest in Kentucky as that which Gosse saw in south Alabama, such as driving the nail and snuffing the candle. He says that in these contests one in three would drive the nail straight, and three out of seven snuffed the candle. Audubon observes that, although the candle-snuffing contest was an exciting sport in itself, it was in reality intended as practice for hunting at night by torchlight. The light not only blinded such animals as deer, bears, wolves, panthers, and bobcats but it made their eyes shine in the darkness, and it was a poor marksman indeed who could not put a bullet between the eyes of his prey.[24]

[22] Philip Henry Gosse, *Letters from Alabama (U.S.) Chiefly Relating to Natural History* (London, 1859), 130–33.

[23] *Ibid.*, 133.

[24] John James Audubon, *Delineation of American Scenery and Character* (with an introduction by Francis H. Herrick) (New York, 1926), 59–62. See also James Hall, *Letters from the West, Containing Sketches of Scenery, Manners and Customs* (London, 1828), 86, for a discussion of the use of the rifle by the common folk; and Arthur, *Western North Carolina,* 252, for a discussion of fire or torchlight hunting.

The average skill as marksmen was in every respect equalled and even surpassed in the Southerners' skill as horsemen. Everybody—men, women, and children, colored and white—rode horseback or muleback. Ofttimes, too, the women were better riders even than the men; for relying completely on their skill in balancing in a sidesaddle, they jumped their horses over wide ditches and high fences with the men, who sat astride their animals and who could, if necessary, use their knees and both feet to brace with. In any case the horsemanship of the Southerners was of no ordinary quality, a point later to be demonstrated by the country boys in the cavalry of Stuart, Wheeler, Morgan, and Forrest. It was not a matter merely of staying on a horse when at breakneck speed, but also of guiding the mount over ditches, hedges, fences, and through tangled swamps and bogs, so as to prevent the horse from falling or injuring himself and rider. Outside of the fox hunt, in which the women of the well-to-do if not those of the poorer folk took part, the public exhibitions of horsemanship were confined to the men. One of the commonest exhibitions of this skill was the "gander pulling," which was probably of European origin. In preparation for the contest a path was laid out in a circle of about 150 or 160 feet in diameter, over which a slack cord was suspended between two poles on each side of the path. A live gander with his neck thoroughly greased was then suspended by his feet from this cord, so as to hang just over the path. The contestants, after depositing a stipulated sum of money as a sweepstake, mounted their horses and rode around the circle a few times in a sort of rehearsal. Then when the signal was given, the riders advanced, three abreast "each fixing his eye steadily upon the gander's shining neck, which he must seize and drag from the body of the wretched bird before the purse is won." When the riders are within about six paces of the suspended fowl, their trouble begins. The gander is frantically darting his snake-like neck in every direction, flapping his wings in a partially successful effort to fly, thus causing the slack cord to swing in a wide arc. At this point two men, "armed with stout whips," standing on each side of the path, flay the riders' horses unmercifully. The horses bound forward, upward, and sidewise all in one frantic effort. To seize and hold the gander's slippery neck with three horses cavorting madly and three men reaching out at about the same time to grasp that neck was a supreme test of equestrian skill and co-ordination of hand and eye.[25]

The singing schools and the community, or all-day singings, were among the most enjoyable of the social institutions of the Southern folk. Every summer usually in one of the neighborhood churches, a singing master would hold a school, which lasted ten days or two weeks. Sometimes two or three singing schools would be held, especially where there were rival singing masters. The business of learning to sing by note was direct and simple; and anyone with any musical talent could, under a competent leader, learn to read notes and to sing by note by the time the school ended. The seven-shaped note system or the five-note system of the Sacred Harp was used. The names and relative positions of these shaped notes were first learned; then followed in rapid succession note values—whole, half, quarter, etc.—sharps and flats, rest, repeats, majors and minors, crescendo and diminuendo, and the four traditional parts, bass, alto, soprano, and tenor.

Learning these elementary principles, however, was only

[25] George W. Featherstonhaugh, "A Canoe Voyage up the Minay Sotor," 196 (MS. copy in the Alabama Department of Archives and History), 13–14; also quoted in Tate, *History of Pickens County, Georgia,* 62.

one phase and not the most enjoyable one of a singing school. A good portion of the day would therefore be taken up with singing well-known sacred and popular songs, and enjoying prolonged recesses devoted to courting, and having a generally sociable time. In the general singing, and even in the teaching, the benches were drawn up in a square with the master in the center and those singing bass, alto, soprano, and tenor in separate sections.

The singing school, though an end in itself, was also the chief means of teaching the people to sing, a thing which they did often and long. At church, prayer meetings, the Sunday-afternoon singings of the younger people, and the all-day singings with dinner on the grounds, people met and sang together.

The all-day singing and dinner on the grounds was an event of such importance that people came from afar to take part in it. It was a sing fest for all; it was a picnic of fried chicken, baked ham, turkey, pies, cakes, and other delicacies, where a feast sufficient for hundreds was spread upon tables built beneath the trees. It was unsurpassed as an occasion for relatives and friends to meet and particularly for young men and girls. It was also a day of exciting rivalry between well-known singing masters who took turns in leading the singing; and woe betide the reputation of one who was unable to sing, without rehearsal, any new song suggested by some member of the assembly or by some rival. A tuning fork was often used to get the pitch; but many singers with a sense of absolute pitch discarded such devices to the embarrassment of the less fortunate.[26]

[26] See Ward, *Ward's History of Coffee County, Georgia,* 124; Brewer, "History of Coosa County," 251; H. V. Wooten, Diary, Pt. I, Chap. 2, 1829 (MS. in Alabama Department of Archives and History), for contemporary reference to singing schools. The singing schools and all-day singings were

Of all the social gatherings, the wedding party was the jolliest. Everyone for miles around, colored or white, slave or free, was invited; and only serious illness or disaster of earthquake dimensions could prevent people from attending. Why not? For a wedding party combined about all the good features of every form of merrymaking. It could at times be a hunting party for the older men and a quilting party for the older women; it was a courting marathon for the young men and young ladies; it was a yarn-swapping contest for the old men; it was a continuous feast of the choicest of food, cooked by women who knew the art of cooking; it was always a dancing party after the wedding; and it was many other things too numerous to catalogue, all of which were somewhat livened by the "flowing bowl," or, more accurately, the gurgling jug. Although such occasions were often marked by uproarious hilarity, they were seldom disturbed by quarrels and personal encounters. But why not let a member of one of these wedding parties describe one? The most detailed account that I have yet read of such an occasion is that written by Dr. H. V. Wooten in his diary. The wedding was that of the niece of Wooten's brother-in-law, John Lodge, which took place at Lodge's house in February, 1829. Wooten had been asked by the bride to be an attendant in the wedding. Though he was to become a prominent physician in later years, at this time he was an awkward, sixteen-year-old lad of the backwoods of Burke County, Georgia; and when the wedding day came, he was "all embarrassed," as he puts it, "and drunk with anticipation." His excitement was increased by the "many girls [who] were in attendance for sometime before, assisting in the preparation" for the wedding, and by the

---

very popular during the boyhood of the present writer and are still held in certain rural communities.

fact that he was the only eligible young man present at first. "On the wedding day after dinner time (I eat [sic] none) I repaired to my room," writes Wooten, "and fixed out, to go and escort the bride groom to his 'lovely fair.' After I had 'rigged out,' I called in my mother who pronounced all right,—and then gave me a charge how to proceed in the duties of my office. I memorized it—all as well as I could, and put out. I found the young man dressing out, his other attendant with him. Soon a goodly company was collected to accompany him. Just about starting time, there came a good rain to lay the dust. This however somewhat disconcerted the party as it was thought that it would prevent many from going, and it was desirable to have a jolly company. The rain stopping we all mounted, the groom and his attendants in front abreast (this was the fashion in those days) [and] we rode on, now and then falling in with others, until we came nearly in sight of home. When we stoped [sic] to 'fix up' here, a consultation rose as to the gait we should move in our approach, [and] it was soon decided that a gallop was decidedly the most graceful and courtly, so we arranged ourselves and charged up. Here indeed was a scene. During my short absence a large concourse of people had assembled. The men of riper years were in groups about the yard talking over the farming business; the young beaux were stroling [sic] about in burning impatience for the company to mix, while a few old white heads were setting [sic] in the big room around the fire, talking of 'old times.' The ladies, many of them, were seated round the room, in prim array, the younger ones looking out at the windows. . . . The whole of the exterior yard fence was covered with boys, the road was full of gigs, barouches, carriages etc., and the surrounding grove was literally clogged with horses, while just in front of the gate stood some well greased kinky heads, to take the horses of the groom's party.

"Now the bustle commenced, the boys commenced scrambling for the most conspicuous places, and consequently falling off the fence, the men pressed forward in solid crowds, while the women, rather modest to run out, crowded the windows as if to try who could stand pressing best. The windows of the dressing room presented quite a ludicrous spectacle. Many naked necks and shoulders were to be seen, squeezed out, with as much eagerness as if there had been a groom arriving for each and all of them. Indeed everything was literally on tiptoe at our approach. We alighted and pressed our way thro' the crowds to the house, when my trouble commenced again about my white pantaloons [white trousers, says Wooten, were always worn by the wedding party]. It will be remembered that I did not wear them on my ride, as it was a muddy day, but now the time had come that they must be put on, and I could find no room but what the females had crept into, even tho' my cloths [sic] were spread out. . . . After some time dodging about, I appealed to my mother again, who soon put things to right. Finally I got on my white pants and being all ready, we waited on the bride. Here my courage was tried. Indeed, all of us, but my fellow attendant, were intirely [sic] new hands. The chairs were so arranged that each one must sit by his girl, and tho' I had been raised amongst women, this was the first time I had ever seated myself by one. I however looked as wise and easy as I could. . . . But my partner was equally bashful as myself. . . . The ceremony passed off and supper came on. All set [sic] up to the table . . . and we, the attendants, handed round and about the eatables. . . . In the performance of this part, I had need to recollect my mother's charge. I passed thro' the supper scene with only a few little blunders, such as calling Mrs. Miss, spilling part of my cargo now and then, and only once hitting a lady's forehead with the edge of a plate, so that she had a blue spot through the balance of the scene.

"After supper, a play commenced, as fashions run. The plays were various but every one had some kisses in it. I dodged these as long as I could, but finally being hemmed I was compelled to *kiss a girl*, a thing I had never done, but I performed with astonishing grace, and from the moment, fell deadly in love with her, though she was one whom I had before always disliked. In this way the night passed away, many went home but some who lived too far stayed all night; and all the bed rooms being crowded with old women and children, they had to sit up. Most of them however amused themselves by courting . . . until morning. Morning came, the men took a drink, the ladies walked in the garden, and all were soon refreshed.

"About 10 o'clock we all prepared ourselves and rode to the bridegroom's mother's, where we had a sumptuous 'infare,' that is a feast of eating and drinking in further celebration of the marriage. Here as the company had somewhat changed, I was again considerably put to. Hardened, however, by my blunders the over night,—I drove on tolerable until dinner. Now it was the fashion for the bride to sit at one end of the table and the groom at the other, and the attendants also to take their respective ends. So I took my stand at the bride's right hand. Now the rub came! My first job was to carve a fowl. This I had never done only at home, where I felt no restraint; but bad as I was stumped, there was no retreat, so I commenced with a trembling hand and a dull knife, two very awkward instruments. Now it was the fashion to have sundry trimmings and dressing, stoed [*sic*] away around the fowl, on the margin of the dish, and after

I had nearly exhausted my patience in dividing a joint,—I made a desperate effort,—the fowl slipped, and displaced divers eggs etc. into the snow white lap of the blushing bride. She, however, drew her handkerchief over them, and passed it off well, tho' I could not afterwards well recollect what happened about this time. Just after this sad hap, my veteran coleague [sic] (he was an old widower) at the other end turned over a large bowl of 'pie button' [and] thus comforted me much, as I considered him a perfect pattern in these matters.

"With these and a few more blunders the infare past off, and towards night, all the company put off for home, I amongst the rest. The only two girls for whom I contracted a . . . partiality were going on the same road with myself. Finally we came to the fork of the road where there must be a separation. One of the girls, however, was going where I lived, and if I did not go with her, nobody would, so of course I went while the other whom I liked a little the best went on home, a distance of six miles. . . . We finally got home, found . . . none there but the family and amongst them 2 very sick children. These were thought too unwell to leave alone, so I and this kind girl agreed to sit up with them. Finally she commenced nodding—and droping [sic] her head very low. Now considering my lap very spacious I kindly offered it to her as a resting place for her drooping head. She accordingly rested herself on my lap and assumed sleep. This was too much for one of my constitution. To hold such a luscious lump of human sweetness on my own diminutive carcas[s], was indeed a proportion of earthly bliss beyond my capacity to bear. My trembling knees soon called in aid my enthusiastic arms, which grasped the delightful burthen with an uncompromising eagerness! She slept on until I discovered after a while that she was noticing things, when I began to talk or rather to breath[e] out my feelings—I told her I loved her!!! and tho' I had that morning ventured to tell my other love that I thought her 'pretty,' yet this was the first time I had confessed love to female kind. After a while we separated, [but] my professions . . . were warmly reciprocated before we parted; and except in similar cases, I was then at the happiest point of my life." [27]

Thus ended a typical, middle-class, country wedding party, described to us a few years later by a person who participated as an attendant in fourteen other weddings before he was twenty years of age.

There were many other interesting and useful folk customs, such as the community care of the sick, games played at schools and parties, the practical joke, and the tall tale. But further exploration of these matters will not be undertaken here. Let me close, however, with quotations from two persons who were of farmer stock and who as young men had shared in the life of the plain folk. George Brewer, teacher and minister, stated the essence of the life of the plain people: "Those were the days of good neighborship, pleasant friendships, and strong attachments growing out of those frequent social gatherings." [28] Reuben Davis, doctor, lawyer, and political leader of distinction, whose family were plain, homespun farmers, expressed a like sentiment. He wrote that the plain country folk of Tennessee, Alabama, and Mississippi, among whom he had grown up,

[27] H. V. Wooten, Diary, Part I, Chap. 2, pp. 24–35. This portion of the manuscript is a memoir rather than a diary, and it forms an introduction to the diary proper, which Wooten kept after he became a physician in Alabama. I have altered his punctuation, occasionally, in the interest of clearness, and in an attempt to bring some of his endless, loose sentences to a close.

[28] Brewer, "History of Coosa County," 196.

"lived a life of great toil and many privations, but they were eminently social, kindly, and friendly. They practiced the most cordial and unstinted hospitality; and in case of sorrow or sickness, or need of any kind, there was no limit to the ready service rendered by neighbors and friends. In those days, people who lived miles apart, counted themselves as neighbors, and even strangers soon became friends. There was this great advantage: that, while none were very wealthy, few were poor enough to suffer actual want." [29]

[29] Reuben Davis, *Recollections of Mississippi and Mississippians.* (Boston, 1889), 3–4.

CHAPTER IV

The Role of the Plain Folk

THE ROLE of the Southern folk was scarcely that of a supernumerary in any phase of Southern life. To deal with them—as has been the tendency in studying the plantation economy—either as a formless mass or filler that settles into the cracks and crevices left by the planters is to take a narrow and incomplete view of Southern society. On the other hand to deal with the plain folk as a class-conscious group, bitter and resentful toward the aristocracy because of exploitation and neglect of the latter, is even farther from reality.

The Southern folk were, as has been repeatedly said, a closely knit people; but they were not class conscious in the Marxian sense, for with rare exceptions they did not regard the planters and men of wealth as their oppressors. On the contrary, they admired them as a rule and looked with approval on their success; and they assumed, on the basis of much tangible evidence, that the door of economic opportunity swung open easily to the thrust of their own ambitious and energetic sons and daughters. Indeed, it was considered a common occurrence outside the older states of Virginia and the Carolinas, for the rank and file to move upward in the economic scale, and for individuals in every community to become well-to-do planters, political leaders, and members of a learned profession. Relatively few of the plain folk, however, seem to have had a desire to become wealthy. Their ambition was to acquire land and other property sufficient to give them and their children a sense of security and well-being, to be "good livers" and "have something saved for a rainy day" as they would have put it. Nevertheless, the knowledge that the economic door was not bolted against themselves and their children tended to stifle the development of a jealous and bitter class consciousness.

The abundance of cheap land, the generally high prices received for farm products and livestock, and the rapidly developing political democracy were the principal means of keeping the economic door unlocked, and preventing the development of a sense of frustration and resentment against the more wealthy. There were, also, other important forces that diminished the feeling of class stratification and helped in the creation of a sense of unity between the plain folk and the aristocracy. Such were the association of rich and poor in all religious activities and in the schools, the frequent ties of blood kinship between them, and the generally folkish and democratic bearing of the aristocracy. This sense of unity between all social and economic groups can not be stressed too much, in view of the strongly and widely held opinion to the contrary. Indeed, when the entire social and economic structure of the Old South is placed in perspective, rather than viewing each segment as a separate thing, all parts will be seen as bearing a relation to the whole. It is then that the plain folk appear not as supernumeraries but as a vital element of the social and economic structure of the Old South. A grazing and farm economy rather than a plantation economy was practiced by nearly all the nonslaveholders and by 60 to 80 per cent of the slaveholders. Farm economy meant a diversified, self-sufficient type of agriculture, where the money crops were subordinated to food crops, and where the labor was performed by the family or the family aided by a few slaves. Plantation economy depended upon slave labor, and usually specialized in the production of one or more of the staple crops, such as cotton, sugar cane, rice, and tobacco. Food crops and livestock were not neglected, as a rule, by the planters; in fact, they frequently produced enough corn for their own use, but such crops were generally subordinated to the money crops. As a result of the self-sufficiency of farm economy, the farmers were seldom involved in indebtedness, once they had paid for their lands.

Farm economy, together with livestock grazing, not only furnished support for the farmers and herdsmen who composed the bulk of the Southern population but supplied a large portion of the hogs, cattle, and breadstuffs purchased for the plantations. Indeed, the farmers and graziers could have easily supplied the entire needs of the South for beef and pork, had not the greater portion of the cattle and hogs been driven to the seaports such as Philadelphia, Baltimore, Charleston, Savannah, Mobile, and New Orleans, where they were usually slaughtered and shipped to the Eastern markets or to the West Indies. Why these cattle and hogs were thus disposed of instead of being sold directly to the planters is a question that can be answered perhaps by a careful study of the weather map. The warm and damp winters of the lower South caused meat to spoil quickly and rendered large-scale slaughter and preservation of meat on the plantations a hazardous business, with the result that the larger drovers could not depend on the plantation markets. The planters often complained in their diaries and letters of their meat supply being spoiled by warm weather. For example Mrs. C. C. Clay of Huntsville, Alabama, wrote her husband on December 5, 1828, that "Augustine has gone to Tennessee in quest of pork. The weather bids fair for the same difficulty to exist in keeping pork that there was last year." On January 7, 1845, over sixteen years later, Mrs. Clay's son, Hugh Lawson Clay, writes his mother that "the weather is bad, very bad, warm and rainy—fair for spoiling pork and for nothing else. Many persons I hear have already lost most of their meat and are unable to buy more." [1] Because of this condition the seaport towns frequently had equipment for the slaughter of animals and the preservation of meat. Such places furnished a more reliable market, where the drovers could dispose of all their cattle and hogs at once instead of peddling them to the planters who might decide not to buy at all. In case such seaport towns were not satisfactorily equipped for slaughtering animals the livestock could be sent to Philadelphia, Baltimore, and Charleston, where they would be slaughtered and packed. It is not at all improbable that much of the meat of Southern livestock was sold back to the Southern planters; indeed, there is a tradition that such was the case. Other raw products such as cotton were treated in this fashion.

The Southern folk, with a more balanced economy than that of the planter groups, were obviously a source of strength when the Civil War came. Frequently all their men—including the heads of families—from 17 to 50 were in military service; but the younger children—boys and girls—the women, and the older men took the place of the absent men in the work and management of the farm. The plantations, however, were not as dependable as the farms

[1] Clay Papers (Duke University Library, Durham, N.C.). Similar references are found in many of the Clay Papers.

in wartime because the slaves—except the house servants —usually fled to the Union lines as soon as the invading army came within reach, and thus completely paralyzed further agricultural production. The farms, on the other hand, continued to operate provided the farmers had been able to conceal their work stock from the Union troops, which was probably not difficult in a country so heavily wooded as the South.

It was, however, during the Reconstruction period that the plain folk revealed their real vitality and power of survival. Accustomed to every phase of work in any way related to farming and rural life, and often frontier life, they had no such readjustment to make as the planter who had usually little manual skill or experience in manual labor. With an ax, saw, auger, frow, drawing knife, and hammer, which might be assembled by a neighborhood pool, the farmers held their house-raisings and rebuilt with logs their houses and barns that had been burned during the war. With a sledge hammer and anvil they fashioned crude plows and hoes from the worn-out parts of old implements or from scrap iron and steel gathered here and there. They built crude wagons and carts, made horse collars by platting shucks, fashioned harness from hickory saplings with ax and drawing knife, and made traces and other parts of the harness from old pieces of chain or home-tanned leather. Often there would be a shortage of work stock, in which case what few old animals that were left would be passed around from place to place until they were unable to go. In some cases on record, men hitched themselves to the plow. In this way the plain folk by ingenuity, heartbreaking toil, patient endurance, self-denial, and physical toughness were able to survive the Civil War and Reconstruction, and restore their farm economy—a vital portion of South-

ern economy. This was accomplished when the plantation
system was in shambles or severely crippled from the dev-
astation of war and the destruction of the slave-labor
system. It is not too much to say that the plain folk thus
rescued the South from complete and, perhaps, final ruin
with little or no aid or sympathy from any sources whatso-
ever outside the borders of their own section.

At this point I wish to say something about the role of
the plain folk in political affairs, but space will permit of
only a few general observations. Did the planter class as
such dominate politics and determine the policy of government to the extent that has been usually claimed? If so,
how did they control the mass of voters? Was it done by
intimidation through threat of physical violence to the
voter or his family?—a method quite common in Europe,
today, and in many organizations in the United States.
Such intimidation as a means of vote getting can of course
be dismissed. It would have been physical and political
suicide in a country where family ties and kinships were
so numerous and close, and where such a threat would have
been enthusiastically met—more than halfway—by men
and boys handy with firearms. Did the aristocracy control
the people by means of economic coercion? This also is a
method too well known in the United States even to be
discussed. This type of coercion was not possible in the
antebellum South, however, since the Southern farmer
usually owned his farm and was dependent on no one. All
forms of coercion were in fact out of keeping with the character of either the common folk or the planters. What of
the use of money to purchase votes necessary to win the
election? Although there must have been in every community individuals whose vote could be purchased, there
is no evidence of a widespread use of bribery to sway the

vote of the people. Besides this, too, was not in keeping with the character of either group. Reuben Davis says in his *Recollections of Mississippi* that "there was little trickery and no corruption in the politics of those days, and a man who had dared tamper with a ballot box, or who had been detected in any fraud by the people, would have been torn in pieces without a moment's hesitation. The populace might be ignorant of many things, careless and indifferent about many more; but where honor and honesty were concerned the great heart of the masses beat true and fearless. Any man who aspired to lead them must be above reproach according to their standards.

"These standards were high enough and clean enough to force aspirants for leadership to at least outward conformity with the popular ideal, and the very existence of such an ideal kept the political atmosphere in a measure pure." [2] The truth of the matter is that whatever influence the planters exercised over the political action of the common people was of a personal and local nature. It was based upon the respect the plain folk of a community had for the character and judgment of individual planters in that community and such qualities of character and judgment in the planter were revealed only by his genuine participation in community affairs.

It must be remembered, however, that there were few genuine planters outside the black belt, and that such personal influence and leadership was relatively narrow. If the farmers who lived outside the black belt were to be brought to support the interest of the planters, a less personal means of gaining their votes would have to be used; and this method had to be that of persuasion. Such persuasion was then as now the chief business of the politicians; and unless

[2] Davis, *Recollections of Mississippi and Mississippians*, 112.

the politicians were planters—and most, except on the national scale, were not—it would immediately become very much of a question as to whose interest was being served, whether that of the planters, or of the plain folk, or of the politicians and their political organizations.

The persuasive efforts made by both Whig and Democratic political leaders to win the political support of the rank and file was extraordinary. The two parties regarded few towns as too small for the establishment of rival newspapers. It was not uncommon for towns of less than one thousand people to have two ably edited newspapers, whose emphasis would be political.[3]

Joint debates were a very popular mode of conducting a campaign. In these debates apt rejoinder, witty repartee and side comments were often more effective than oratory. The common folk loved good oratory, but they revelled in the witty thrust and parry and in the practical joke. William H. Milburn tells of a political speaker, who, as he puts it, "was quite overthrown at the summit of a gorgeous flight of eloquence, and left to slink dumfounded from the stage" when an unscrupulous adversary bawled out at his back "guess he wouldn't talk quite so hifalutenin if he knowed his breeches was torn out behind."[4] These joint debates and political speeches, the one purpose of which was to gain popular support for political candidates, were usually successful in bringing together a great concourse of people. To make sure of a large attendance, scores of hogs, beeves, and young goats were barbecued, and barrels of lemonade were served. Seldom has the suffrage of the common

[3] Lewy Dorman, *Party Politics in Alabama From 1850 Through 1860* (Montgomery, 1935), 19–20.

[4] William H. Milburn, *The Pioneers, Preachers and People of the Mississippi Valley* (New York, 1860), 467.

folk been so courted as in the late antebellum South, and, as a result of this, seldom have the people been so well posted on the political issues of the day. "One of the most remarkable characteristics of the Southern people before the war," observes Reuben Davis, the Mississippi politician, "was their universal enjoyment of public speaking. . . . In consequence of this, the art of fluent speaking was largely cultivated, and a man could hope for little success in public life unless he possessed this faculty in some degree. Another consequence was that there was never a people better educated on political questions than the Southerners of that day." [5]

The significance of the role of the plain folk in politics may be partly evaluated from some of the provisions of the new state constitutions adapted under popular pressure between 1830 and 1860. Universal white manhood suffrage, the popular election of virtually all county and state officers, and the abolition of property qualifications for office holding in most cases were good examples. If the Democratic party, as it has been constantly asserted, was primarily the agency of the common people and the Whig party that of the planters and business interests, then more often than not in the lower South, at least, the party of wealth took a beating. Nor were the Democrats at all tenderhearted in the methods. In Alabama, for example, a Democratic legislature abolished the use of the three-fifths ratio in the election of Congressmen and placed representation thus on the white basis. This greatly reduced the power of the black belt, which was the Whig stronghold, and gave the white counties control. This law was followed by the reapportionment act of 1843 which gerrymandered the Congressional districts so as to insure the continued control of the white

[5] Davis, *Recollections of Mississippi and Mississippians,* 69.

counties. Then in the session of 1855-1856 the Democratic legislature in a redistricting act gerrymandered the Whig districts still further; and although the Whigs had an estimated 45 per cent of the population of the state they were able to elect only two Congressmen out of the seven under this act.[6] Finally it was the Democratic party which took the lead in the secession of the Southern states. The Whig planters and businessmen generally were opposed to secession until the last and went out of the Union reluctantly.

Reference has been frequently made to the fact that outside the older states, individuals were constantly rising from the farmer to the planter class. There are indications, in fact, that in some areas a majority had thus risen from relative poverty as had the older planter class in the seaboard states. Much depended on when the immigrant settled, as was pointed out in discussing migration. Settlers on rich soils usually rose more rapidly and further than those on poorer soils. Indeed, it appears that in many parts of the black belt most of the settlers were either nonslaveholders or small slaveholders, and that frequently both nonslaveholders and small slaveholders became large slaveholders.

But the plain folk made a much larger contribution to the leadership in other classes than they did to that of the planter class. It appears to be true in the lower South and in Tennessee and Kentucky that the bulk of lawyers, physicians, preachers, editors, teachers, businessmen, and political leaders below the national level were members of fam-

[6] Dorman, *Party Politics in Alabama*, 25–26, 96–99. The development of political democracy is ably treated in Charles S. Sydnor, *The Development of Southern Sectionalism, 1819–1848* (Vol. V of *A History of the South*) (Baton Rouge, 1948), Chaps. II and XII; and in Fletcher M. Green, "Democracy in the Old South," *Journal of Southern History*, XII (1946), 1–23.

ilies who were poor or only comfortably well off. A young man of ability, energy, and determination—barring unusually bad luck—could scarcely fail of considerable success in any of the professions. He might never set the world on fire—in fact, he probably would have no such desire as a rule—but he could nearly always rise to local leadership. After examining the life histories of a large number of individuals who have risen from obscurity and comparative poverty, one cannot fail to see that they all follow a similar pattern. First, the parents, though often very poor, usually possessed education beyond the limits of mere literacy and had great respect for education as a means of attaining success. Then, too, they had a certain refinement, which their robust neighbors did not usually have. Not that they were aloof or prideful in their bearing; only they nursed a spark in their bosoms which they were able to pass on to some of their children. Next the son, or sons, who felt this spark of pride and ambition, utilized all possible opportunities at home and at school to acquire education. After he had acquired sufficient education and age he would teach school, clerk in a store, or find other employment which would enable him to save enough money to attend the academy or even college. Apparently most young men of this type taught school. The third step was the preparation for his profession, usually the law, medicine, or the ministry.

If he were to be a lawyer, ofttimes he read law under the direction of an attorney while teaching school, though occasionally he would attend a law school. When he had been admitted to the bar he would usually enter a law office in a minor capacity—frequently as a sort of secretary and copyist for the firm. If he were shrewd and energetic—and young men of this type usually were—he would soon rise into a prominent position in the firm or as an independent

attorney. The essentials to success were a practical knowledge of the law, an understanding of country jurors, some
oratorical talent, and, always, cleverness in debate and
repartee. There was much legal business in the rural South
and a lawyer of only modest talent could earn a good in-
come. Such well-known Georgians as Charles Tait, United
States Senator and Federal Judge; William H. Crawford,
United States Senator and Secretary of the Treasury;
Richard Henry Wilde, State Attorney General and Congressman; William Towne, Congressman and Governor;
Joseph E. Brown, Governor, Judge, and United States
Senator; Alexander H. Stephens, Congressman, Vice-
President of the Confederacy, and Governor, followed the
pattern sketched above. Indeed, says W. H. Sparks, from
the ranks of the poor but ambitious youth "arose most of
those men so distinguished in her Georgia's earlier history." [7]

If the young man planned to become a physician, his
preparation could be as little or as much as he desired and
was able to pay for. The commonest procedure even for
the most ambitious was to obtain employment with a prac-
ticing physician—such as keeping his books, driving his
buggy, and running errands. In his spare time, if any, the
apprentice read the medical books in the doctor's office and
perhaps dissected a cadaver—at least for a while, until it
spoiled completely. The doctor, no doubt, on his long drives
would teach his assistant, as best he could, the knotty
problems in his books and in his practice. After two or three

[7] Sparks, *Memories of Fifty Years*, 117–18. The best sources for the study
of leadership in the learned professions in the antebellum South are county
and local histories, memoirs and autobiographies of lawyers, physicians,
and preachers, and the state histories of religious denominations and of the
bench and bar. Many such sources have been examined in this study, and
only general reference is made here to this type of material.

years of this apprenticeship, the student doctor could with no real difficulty obtain license to practice; in fact, he could without much risk set up most anywhere and practice without license. Perhaps the majority of apprentice physicians did not end their studies at this point but went off for a course of lectures and study in a medical college, which would extend over a period varying from a few months to several years.

Often, however, a poor young man planning to be a physician taught school or clerked in a store, just as had the prospective lawyer, for the purpose of saving enough money to complete his academic education and pay his expenses in a medical school.

An examination of the life histories of large numbers of the clergy seems to indicate that an overwhelming majority were recruits from the ranks of the people, and that they acquired their education in a fashion similar to that of the young men preparing for the other professions. Many began their careers as schoolmasters and, indeed, many continued throughout life to teach school.

The life histories of those who entered business, such as banking, merchandising and real estate (better known as "land speculation") are not as well known as are those of men who entered one of the learned professions. The cases which have been examined, however, indicate that, although the field was more limited in the South than those of planting and the professions, the percentage of those from the ranks of the common folk was high.

Since education was for the poor but ambitious youth the gateway to success in business and the professions, what were the opportunities for acquiring the necessary education? Much has been said and even more has been assumed, and therefore implied, to the effect that the educational institutions of the South were practically closed to all but the well-to-do because of the great expense of attending them. It is certainly not my purpose to go into the history and theory of education in the Old South, but I will briefly point out a few facts which may indicate that the obstacles to acquiring an education were not very great if an education was desired.

The first thing is to observe that the common folk of the South obviously received relatively more schooling than has generally been supposed. By comparing the illiteracy of the Southern people with that of the people of New England, where for well-known reasons a common school system had long existed, the South has been made to appear as a land where mass ignorance prevailed. In 1850, for example, the census showed that only 1.89 per cent of the white population of New England above twenty years of age could not read; but in the South 8.27 per cent of this age group were illiterate. The fact was not advertised, however, that in the Northwest, where population was sparse and scattered somewhat as in the rural South 5.03 per cent of those above twenty were illiterate.

Just how illiterate, however, is the 8.27 per cent of the South and the 5.03 per cent of the Northwest? The answer is that in comparison with the situation in most countries of the world at that time the Southern folk were one of the most literate major groups of the entire world. In 1846, for example, of all the couples throughout England and Wales who got married, 32.6 per cent of the men and 48.1 per cent of the women affixed their marks instead of their signatures to applications for licenses. In the French army in 1851, of 311,218 conscripts 34 per cent could neither read nor write. The marriage and conscription records are very good cross sections of the young adult population; but in both France and England the young people were more literate than the older groups because of the improvement of the common school systems. In Spain, Portugal, Italy, the Balkans, Poland, and Russia illiteracy was between 90 and 95 per cent. Only in the Scandinavian countries, Belgium, and Holland, Prussia, and Saxony was the literacy of the people comparable with or greater than that of the South.[8] Most of the children in the rural communities of the South, including those of the well-to-do, learned to read and write and cypher in the old field schools. These were elementary schools, in which reading and writing and arithmetic and sometimes higher subjects were taught. They were financed primarily by subscription, each child being charged about two and one half dollars for a five or six months' term and one dollar for a six-week summer session. Toward the end of the period, many of these schools were receiving aid from both the state and county. Most of the academies, which will be discussed presently, had primary departments that taught the same things as the old field schools. The academies were usually located in a town or village.

Literacy is not education; however, if college attendance is any test of an educated people, the South had more educated men and women in proportion to population than the North, or any other part of the world. According to the 1860 census, out of a white population of 7,400,000 there were 25,882 students enrolled in Southern colleges, whereas in the North, with a white population of over 19,000,000, there were only 27,408 students in college; and

[8] J. D. B. DeBow, *Statistical View of the United States Census . . . Being a Compendium of the Seventh Census* (Washington, 1854), 148–49.

quite a large number of these were from the South. That is, there was one college student for each 247 white persons in the South and one in 703 in the North.

It was, however, the academy more than the colleges that gave the poor but ambitious youth their education. There were at the end of the antebellum period about 2,500 academies in the South. Most had primary departments to take care of the youngsters of the town and vicinity; they all had what would have been called high-school subjects, many of which are now taught in college; and all the larger, better equipped offered college work.

The tuition in these academies, most of which had ten-month sessions was low—about what the library, contingent, and athletic fee is in most of the schools today. The tuition per annum in the 57 academies of Georgia in 1860 averaged $15.50 for the elementary branches and in the higher branches $26.00.[9] A study of over a score of academies in Alabama shows that the tuition for a student ranged from $15 to $25 in the primary departments and $25 to $35 in the high schools. Those academies that gave college work usually charged $40 to $50 a year. Board, room, and laundry ranged from eight to ten dollars per month. In short, for less than $150 a young man or young lady could attend an academy for ten months.[10]

[9] *A Gazetteer of Georgia, Containing a Particular Description of the State* (4th ed.; Macon, 1860), 143–48.

[10] The contemporary local newspapers contain much information about the academies, both in their advertisements and in their news and editorial columns. The county and town histories usually carry considerable information about the academies. The following works are useful in this connection: Edgar Knight, *Public Education in the South* (Boston, 1922); M. C. S. Noble, *History of the Public Schools of North Carolina* (Chapel Hill, 1930); Charles W. Dabney, *Universal Education in the South*, 2 vols. (Chapel Hill, 1936); Robert H. White, *Development of the Tennessee State Educational Organization, 1796–1929* (Kingsport, Tenn., 1929);

Of course the quality of work offered by the academies varied with the quality of teachers and equipment. Edgar Knight in his *Public Education in the South* says that "the academy was a very highly respected means of education in the South, where it extended in greater numbers than in any other section of the country." [11]

The following subjects were usually taught in the academies: Elementary—spelling, reading, writing, arithmetic, English grammar, and geography. High School—chemistry, logic, ethics or moral philosophy, psychology (called intellectual science), physics, astronomy, political economy, composition and rhetoric, Greek, Latin, French, algebra, geometry, trigonometry, mechanical drawing, analytical geometry and calculus (by request). In the female academies, drawing, painting, fine needlework, and music were always offered, the tuition being extra. All of these, of course, were not required; in fact, a student could take one or all of them as it suited him or his purse. The struggling country youth eager to acquire an education would take every course possible.

It thus appears that the opportunity of acquiring an education—the gateway to the professions and to success was quite favorable for the ambitious youth, however poor he might be. Indeed, it can be rather positively asserted that most young men, at least, who *desired* an education, could obtain one. The catchword, let it be observed, is *desired*. Aye! There was the rub!—and it still is!

---

and I. M. E. Blandin, *History of Higher Education of Women in the South Prior to 1860* (New York, 1909).

[11] Knight, *Public Education in the South*, 73.

APPENDIX

CHAPTER V

A Statistical Analysis of Land and Slave Holdings in Sample Counties

IN A PRECEDING chapter it was indicated that a statistical analysis of landownership would be presented at this point. The two chief sources for this analysis are the county tax lists and the manuscript census reports. The tax lists are, quite naturally, more accurate as a rule than the census reports; for the tax officer was collecting *money*, while the census taker was collecting *names*. But complete reliance upon the tax lists as the basic source for the study of landownership is not possible because of the fact that in many large areas of the South those antebellum records have perished.[1] We are therefore thrown back upon the census reports as the basic statistical source, except in a few areas where the census returns for the "Productions of Agriculture" have been lost or destroyed and the tax lists have survived. Even in the census material, we are circumscribed by the fact that only for the censuses of 1850 and 1860 have

[1] The taxbooks failed to indicate what a person's vocation was, or whether he was the head of a family, and thus made them less valuable as a source in studying land tenure of the agricultural population.

any of the agricultural schedules been preserved. That is to say, our statistical analysis will of necessity have to deal with the latter part of the antebellum period, though occasionally the surviving tax lists may be used to make excursions further into the past. But the last two censuses do give a final picture of the Old South.

There are three schedules of the unpublished census for 1850 and 1860 which contain the data being used in the studies on land tenure and kindred subjects. These are Schedule I, "Free Inhabitants," Schedule II, "Slave Inhabitants," and Schedule IV, "The Productions of Agriculture." Schedule I contains valuable data about every free person, white and colored, in each county of the states and territories of the United States. All persons are arranged in family groups; their ages, trade or profession, nativity by states, and their literacy are given; and the value of the real estate that each person owned is listed opposite his name. Schedule II gives the age, sex, and color of the slaves owned by each operator and lists them all under the names of the owners, so that each individual slaveholder can be identified and the number and types of his slaves determined. Thus slaveholding farmers and planters can be segregated from the nonslaveholding farmers in studying landownership. Schedule IV, "The Productions of Agriculture," contains the names of the farm "operators" but makes no distinction between owners and tenants. This schedule, however, contains a wealth of information: the amount of improved and unimproved land under the control of each farm operator—whether owner or tenant—the number, description, and value of livestock; an itemized statement of the chief agricultural productions of the farm; the value of home manufactures—and some other information—are given for each farm and farmer.

By assembling on a master chart the relevant information from these three schedules under the names of the heads of each farm family, a reasonably accurate basis for a study of land tenure may be established. Landowners can be separated from renters; slaveholding landowners can be separated from nonslaveholding landowners; and the sizes of most holdings can be analyzed. The process is simple, but exceedingly tedious and long-drawn-out, for the several schedules are located at different places. The Census Bureau has retained at Washington Schedules I and II, "Free Inhabitants" and "Slave Inhabitants," while other schedules have been distributed to the states which they cover. Several Southern states, however—Tennessee, Georgia, Florida, Louisiana, Kentucky, and perhaps another one or two—failed to receive these unpublished schedules, and most of them were finally given to Duke University. In order to bring these schedules together for the purpose of obtaining the necessary data from each one we had Schedules I and II (located at Washington) microfilmed. Schedule IV, located in the archives of the states or at Duke University, could not be satisfactorily microfilmed because the data for each farm operator is on the front and back of the same sheet. It has been found necessary, therefore, to copy by hand on a master chart the entire agricultural schedule for each sample county. Each sheet usually contains the names of forty-one operators, and an experienced copyist can transcribe one sheet on an average of about thirty minutes. Many counties have between fifty and one hundred sheets in Schedule IV. The next step is to check the names of the farm operators with the names on the microfilm of Schedule I, "Free Inhabitants" since the latter schedule will indicate whether the operator owned his farm.

The final step in preparing the master chart is to check the names of all farmers and planters against Schedule II to identify nonslaveholders and slaveholders and to determine the number of slaves held by each individual. The master chart is then ready to be transferred, name by name with all data, to punch cards for processing with an electric sorting machine. This being done, an electric calculator is used to work out tables.

This procedure is very slow and tedious, and the life of one person would scarcely be long enough to check and analyze the structure of land and slave ownership and the productions of agriculture in every county of a single large state through two censuses. The best procedure has, therefore, seemed to be one that takes into consideration the finite nature of man's life and the finite quality of the reader's patience with and interest in statistics; and this procedure is to use the sampling method. Sample counties in five Southern states have been used.

In making the analysis of the structure of the ownership of land and slaves, sample counties from the grazing regions and the agricultural zones have been selected. The grazing economy, as previously observed, was practiced in the great pine belt and mountains; and agriculture was the principal occupation of the people in the more fertile zone, lying between the piney woods and the highlands in the lower South and outside the mountains in the upper central South. The pine belt as exemplified in counties from southern Georgia, Alabama, Mississippi, and Louisiana will be examined first. Following that, the agricultural zone of the lower South extending across the same states will be studied. This area will be roughly divided into the uplands and the black belt—the "black belt" is the term applied to the more fertile regions where the Negro population was in the majority. Tennessee has such a variety of topographical and geological areas that it will be dealt with separately.

THE GEORGIA PINE BELT

Georgia has by all odds the largest pine area of any state, and the soil of the south and southeastern part of the state is with some exceptions sandy. In making the statistical analysis of land tenure and slaveownership for this region, four counties of southern Georgia have been selected: Lowndes, Montgomery, Tatnall, and Wayne.

The original census returns for 1860—none for 1850 exist —have been used in making the statistical analysis of landownership and slaveownership for Lowndes and Montgomery; but since the agricultural schedules for Tatnall and Wayne could not be located when the material for Georgia was being assembled, the tax lists for those counties have been used as the main source and the published census as an auxiliary source. The only tax book that approximated the census years of 1850 and 1860 were those of 1844 and 1862 for Wayne, and 1853 and 1860 for Tatnall.

Table IX gives the distribution of landownership in the Georgia piney woods as exhibited in the four counties.

On close examination, this portion of Georgia which was selected by travelers as the peculiar habitat of the poor whites showed complexity. There were, of course, no great fortunes; but, on the other hand, there were well-to-do folk and nearly one third of the farmers were slaveowners, usually small holders. The slaveholders were already placing more emphasis on agriculture than were the nonslaveholders, and this in turn placed more importance upon the ownership of land. Tables X and XI give the distribution of landownership for the nonslaveholders and the slave-holders.

TABLE IX

LANDOWNERSHIP OF THE AGRICULTURAL POPULATION

County	Year	Heads of families engaged in agriculture	Percentage of landowners	Percentage of landless
Lowndes	1860	405	77.28	22.72
Montgomery	1860	340	92.94	7.06
Tatnall	1853	434	81.57	18.43
	1860	551	78.77	21.23
Wayne	1844	162	61.73	38.28
	1862	241	75.93	24.07

TABLE X

LANDOWNERSHIP OF THE SLAVEHOLDING FARMERS

County	Year	Heads of families engaged in agriculture	Percentage of landowners	Percentage of landless
Lowndes	1860	182	95.05	4.95
Montgomery	1860	110	99.10	.90
Tatnall	1853	97	100.00	.00
	1860	158	98.10	1.90
Wayne	1844	50	90.00	10.00
	1862	61	96.72	3.28

TABLE XI

LANDOWNERSHIP OF NONSLAVEHOLDING FARMERS

County	Year	Heads of families engaged in agriculture	Percent- age of landowners	Percent- age of landless
Lowndes	1860	223	62.78	37.22
Montgomery	1860	206	89.96	10.04
Tatnall	1853	337	76.26	23.74
	1860	393	70.99	29.01
Wayne	1844	112	49.11	50.89
	1862	183	67.76	32.24

TABLE XII

SIZES OF HOLDINGS

	THE GEORGIA PINE BELT AS A WHOLE, 1860		TATNALL COUNTY 1860	
	Slave- holding landowners 497	Nonslave- holding landowners 749	Slave- holding landowners 155	Nonslave- holding landowners 279
Acres owned	Percentage of owners	Percentage of owners	Percentage of owners	Percentage of owners
1–50	.80	3.74	—	.36
51–100	1.41	6.01	1.29	3.58
101–200	2.01	9.08	2.58	12.54
201–300	5.23	16.56	1.94	13.98
301–400	4.23	8.14	3.87	11.47
401–500	12.68	17.89	7.10	12.55
501–1,000	21.73	24.83	20.65	31.90
1,001–5,000	47.08	13.80	54.19	13.62
Above 5,000	4.83	—	8.39	—

By 1860 practically all the slaveholders and about 70 per cent of the nonslaveholders owned their land.

The structure of landownership in the Georgia pine region as a whole in 1860 is shown in Table XII made up of the totals of the four sample counties for that date (Wayne, for 1862).

Table XIII, giving the slaveholdings in Tatnall County in 1853, is fairly typical of the pine belt of Georgia in the late antebellum period.

TABLE XIII

SLAVEHOLDING

Tatnall County 1853 Slaves owned	Slaveholders, 158 Percentage of owners
1–5	60.76
6–10	24.68
11–20	10.76
21–30	3.16
31–40	—
41–50	.63

THE ALABAMA PINE BELT

Next in order is the pine region of Alabama. As we have pointed out, although portions of this area were sandy lands, other portions were capable of being utilized for agriculture because of clay subsoil and genuine sandy-loam soil. An examination of the Agricultural Schedule of the last two censuses prior to the Civil War will give evidence of the growing awareness of this fact among the settlers. But, as we have observed, the great yellow-pine forests of Alabama were almost untouched during this period; and the bulk of the inhabitants, though settling down and slowly evolving into agriculturists, were still more dependent upon hunting and the grazing of livestock than upon farming. Three counties have been selected from this piney-woods area, Coffee, Covington, and Washington (though a small portion of Washington is prairie and river bottom), for the purpose of analysis.

Table XIV, calculated upon the basis of the heads of agricultural families as listed in the "Free Inhabitants" Schedules of the census returns of 1850 and 1860, gives the distribution of landownership in the piney woods for those two years.

TABLE XIV

LANDOWNERSHIP OF THE AGRICULTURAL POPULATION

County	Year	Heads of families engaged in agriculture	Percent-age of landowners	Percent-age of landless
Coffee	1850	731	46.24	53.76
	1860	1,116	75.27	24.73
Covington	1850	482	39.83	60.17
	1860	760	68.16	31.84
Washington	1850	259	53.66	46.34
	1860	288	73.96	26.04

It will be observed from Table XIV that, though much of the region was still Federal and state land at the end of the antebellum period, the ownership of land in the piney woods of Alabama was more widely diffused in 1850 than might be expected of a sparsely settled population, still primarily dependent upon a grazing and hunting economy. In each of the sample counties the distribution of the ownership of land had increased during the ten years between 1850 and 1860 from an average of about 45 per cent to about 70 per cent of the farm population. The herdsmen and hunters, who had led a seminomadic life as they drifted southwestward along the great pine zone, were finding it necessary to gain possession of the best agricultural lands for homesteads and to graze their reduced droves of livestock upon a poorer and more limited public range.

The complexity of the piney-woods society continues as exhibited in the older states. Although there were few large slaveholders in this region, there was a considerable body of small slaveholders. The slaveholders were quicker to settle upon their own land than were the nonslaveholders, for the need for large quantities of foodstuffs—corn, sweet potatoes, peas, beans, and rice—was more urgent than in the case of the nonslaveholders. Table XV, below, and Table XVI, on page 161, show what proportion of slaveholders and nonslaveholders owned land in the three sample counties in 1850 and 1860.

TABLE XV

LANDOWNERSHIP OF THE SLAVEHOLDING FARMERS

County	Year	Heads of families engaged in agriculture	Percentage of landowners	Percentage of landless
Coffee	1850	133	67.67	32.33
	1860	198	91.41	8.59
Covington	1850	80	77.50	22.50
	1860	123	91.87	8.13
Washington	1850	109	77.98	22.02
	1860	125	83.20	16.80

In the case of the nonslaveholder in Alabama, the structure of ownership in the piney woods was nearly identical with that in the uplands and black belt of that state and by 1860 strikingly similar to that in the other Federal-land states. Table XVII (the date 1850 is used because the Agricultural Schedule for 1860 which gives the sizes of farms could not be located when these calculations were made) gives a composite picture of the pine belt; that is, the sample counties are thrown together and one county of the region is used as a specific illustration.

As already stated, the census enumerators were instructed not to list a farmer on the Agricultural Schedule unless he produced a certain minimum. Many of the settlers in the piney woods, as observed in the previous chapters, were cultivating only a few acres of land and were, therefore, omitted from the Agricultural Schedule and, consequently, the sizes of their holdings could not be determined exactly. But in the Population Schedule, "Free Inhabitants," we find them classed as "farmers," and the value of the land is given. By comparing the evaluation of their land with that of their neighbors a reasonably accurate estimate of the sizes of their holdings can be made, and it is certain that the bulk of them owned tracts of land ranging from 1 to 200 acres. It appears then, that about 88 per cent of the nonslaveholders who owned land possessed up to 200 acres and the other 12 per cent owned above 200 acres. In the case of the slaveholders it appears that about 56 per cent of the landowners held from 1 to 200 acres.

The pattern of slaveholding in the Alabama pine lands is fairly well illustrated by that of Coffee County. (See Table XVIII, on page 162.)

TABLE XVI

LANDOWNERSHIP OF THE NONSLAVEHOLDING FARMERS

County	Year	Heads of families engaged in agriculture	Percentage of landowners	Percentage of landless
Coffee	1850	598	41.47	58.53
	1860	918	71.79	28.21
Covington	1850	402	32.34	67.66
	1860	637	63.58	36.42
Washington	1850	150	36.00	64.00
	1860	163	66.87	33.13

TABLE XVII

SIZES OF HOLDINGS

	ALABAMA PINE BELT AS A WHOLE, 1850		COFFEE COUNTY 1850	
	Slaveholding landowners 237	Nonslaveholding landowners 432	Slaveholding landowners 90	Nonslaveholding landowners 248
Acres owned	Percentage of owners	Percentage of owners	Percentage of owners	Percentage of owners
1–50	9.70	26.09	12.22	24.19
51–100	14.94	26.34	14.44	34.68
101–200	27.86	24.92	34.44	30.24
201–300	11.47	3.41	14.46	6.85
301–400	7.12	3.78	8.89	2.02
401–500	3.34	2.05	4.44	.40
501–1,000	15.27	1.94	7.78	1.61
1,001–1,500	4.39	—	3.33	—
1,501–2,000	.93	—	—	—
2,001–up	1.96	—	—	—
Not determined	3.37	11.47	—	.01

TABLE XVIII

SLAVEHOLDING

Coffee County 1860 Slaves owned	Slaveholders, 198 Percentage of owners
1–5	61.62
6–10	19.70
11–20	13.13
21–30	3.52
31–40	1.52
41–50	.51

MISSISSIPPI PINE BELT

In 1850 the Mississippi piney woods had a higher percentage of landownership than the Alabama pine belt, due, no doubt, to the recent arrival in the latter region of numerous immigrants, who had not had the time to perfect title to their lands. While the percentage of landownership had greatly increased in Alabama by 1860, nevertheless, Mississippi still remained considerably ahead. Tables XIX, XX, XXI, XXII, XXIII, and XXIV were compiled from the work of Herbert Weaver on land tenure and agriculture in Mississippi.[2] Table XIX—based upon the total number of heads of agricultural families—shows the percentage of landowners in the farm population of the sample piney-woods counties, who owned their homesteads in 1850 and 1860.

Tables XX and XXI show the percentage of slaveholders and nonslaveholders, respectively, who were landowners.

[2] Herbert Weaver, *Mississippi Farmers, 1850–1860* (Nashville, 1945), 66, 67, Tables 10 and 11, pp. 81–82, and Table 5, p. 39, respectively.

TABLE XIX

LANDOWNERSHIP OF THE AGRICULTURAL POPULATION

County	Year	Heads of families engaged in agriculture	Percentage of landowners	Percentage of landless
Harrison	1850	166	68.07	31.93
	1860	112	74.11	25.58
Jones	1850	297	93	7
	1860	435	87	13
Scott	1850	350	78	22
	1860	777	73	27
Wayne	1850	267	66	34
	1860	248	77	23

TABLE XX

LANDOWNERSHIP OF THE SLAVEHOLDING FARMERS

County	Year	Heads of families engaged in agriculture	Percentage of landowners	Percentage of landless
Harrison	1850	57	85.96	14.04
	1860	35	97.14	2.86
Jones	1850	53	100.	—
	1860	94	100.	—
Scott	1850	142	92.96	7.04
	1860	326	87.73	12.27
Wayne	1850	107	95.33	4.67
	1860	61	91.80	8.20

TABLE XXI

LANDOWNERSHIP OF THE NONSLAVEHOLDING FARMERS

County	Year	Heads of families engaged in agriculture	Percent-age of landowners	Percent-age of landless
Harrison	1850	109	58.72	41.28
	1860	77	63.34	36.36
Jones	1850	244	91.39	8.61
	1860	341	83.28	16.72
Scott	1850	208	68.27	31.73
	1860	451	62.08	37.92
Wayne	1850	160	48.88	51.12
	1860	187	72.73	27.27

TABLE XXII

SIZES OF HOLDINGS

	MISSISSIPPI PINE BELT AS A WHOLE, 1850		SCOTT COUNTY 1850	
	Slave-holding landowners 336	Nonslave-holding landowners 504	Slave-holding landowners 132	Nonslave-holding landowners 142
Acres owned	Percentage of owners	Percentage of owners	Percentage of owners	Percentage of owners
1–49	17.56	62.10	15.15	45.77
50–99	13.69	12.50	9.85	11.97
100–199	14.88	10.32	10.61	19.01
200–299	10.41	2.58	13.64	5.63
300–399	11.01	1.19	12.12	1.41
400–499	5.65	1.39	7.58	.70
500–599	10.41	.99	10.61	2.82
1,000–4,999	8.63	.40	12.12	1.41
5,000 and over	.55	—	.76	—
Not determined	6.39	8.50	7.58	11.27

Table XXII shows the landownership structure of both the nonslaveholders and slaveholders in the Mississippi pine belt in 1850. As was done in the case of Alabama, a picture of the region as a whole will be given, and one county typical of the region will be used as a specific example.

The patterns of landownership in the Mississippi and Alabama piney woods were quite dissimilar in 1850. In Mississippi about 63 per cent of the nonslaveholders who owned land possessed small tracts ranging from 50 acres down, while in Alabama over 70 per cent of this group owned over 50 acres, indeed at least a third owned over 100 acres. The explanation lies in the fact that the piney-woods folk of Mississippi were still primarily livestock graziers and hunters, whose chief interest in the ownership of land was to have a place for a cabin, a few outhouses and stock pens, and corn and truck patches. Those in Alabama were placing a great deal more emphasis upon farming, which carried with it the need of owning larger bodies of land than when the grazing of cattle overshadowed all agricultural pursuits.

In 1860, however, the structure of landownership in the Mississippi pine belt was becoming similar to that of Alabama with the result that the bulk of both slaveholders and nonslaveholders owned above one hundred acres rather than below fifty acres as in 1850. An examination of the Agricultural Schedule shows, by the increased amount of improved land as well as greater agricultural production, that the settlers were slowly decreasing their herds and increasing their fields.

Table XXIII gives the structure of landownership of slaveholders and nonslaveholders in 1860.

The pattern of slaveholding in the Mississippi pine region corresponded very closely to that in the pine zone of the

TABLE XXIII

Sizes of Holdings

| | MISSISSIPPI PINE BELT AS A WHOLE, 1860 | | SCOTT COUNTY 1860 | |
| | Slave-holding landowners 470 | Nonslave-holding landowners 749 | Slave-holding landowners 286 | Nonslave-holding landowners 280 |
Acres owned	Percentage of owners	Percentage of owners	Percentage of owners	Percentage of owners
1–49	3.40	17.75	3.15	11.07
50–99	8.30	16.69	8.04	23.57
100–199	15.74	23.49	17.48	32.50
200–299	14.68	13.48	16.08	12.86
300–399	13.19	9.47	13.29	8.21
400–499	10.21	3.74	10.84	2.14
500–999	18.51	5.47	16.78	3.93
1,000–4,999	11.28	.69	12.24	0.36
5,000 and over	1.06	.27	.70	—
Not determined	3.62	10.94	1.40	5.36

TABLE XXIV

Slaveholding

Scott County

| | 1850 Slaveholders 132 | 1860 Slaveholders 286 |
Slaves owned	Percentage of owners	Percentage of owners
1–4	52.72	35.68
5–9	18.97	21.40
10–19	21.08	12.99
20–29	4.21	6.12
30–39	1.40	22.93
40–49	.71	.51
50–99	.71	.51

other Southern states. Table XXIV of slaveholdings in Scott County presents a picture fairly typical of the piney-woods region of Mississippi.

LOUISIANA PINE BELT AND PRAIRIES

While Louisiana has less piney woods than most of the lower Southern states, some parishes lying adjacent to the Mississippi pine lands just discussed belong in this class. Likewise in southwest Louisiana there is a body of pine land that juts out into the edges of the open prairies. The grazing and hunting economy predominated in the piney woods and prairies. Harry L. Coles has analyzed four of these piney-woods and prairie parishes with reference to the distribution of the ownership of land and slaves and the sizes of holdings and Table XXV, page 168, is based on his analysis.[3]

The distribution of the ownership of farm lands was, with the exception of Sabine Parish, wider than in any other grazing region thus far examined. The Louisiana prairies and, perhaps, the piney woods were superior ranges to those in the other states; and the settlers in these regions during the last ten years of the antebellum period, felt it to be imperative as graziers to secure a homestead as a base of operation for their herds and for subsistence. Table XXVI, page 168, and Table XXVII, page 169, taken from Coles's study, analyze the sizes of farms of the heads of families in the piney woods and prairie region in 1860.

Tables XXVI and XXVII reveal that in 1860 the piney woods of east Louisiana and the adjoining pine region of Mississippi had similar patterns of ownership, and that

---

[3] "Some Notes on Slaveownership and Landownership, 1850–1860" in *Journal of Southern History*, IX (1943), 381–94.

TABLE XXV

LANDOWNERSHIP OF THE AGRICULTURAL POPULATION

Parish	Year	Heads of families engaged in agriculture	Percentage of landowners	Percentage of landless
Washington	1850	267	81	19
	1860	446	75	25
Calcasieu	1850	330	82	18
	1860	290	97	3
Sabine	1850	591	39	61
	1860	530	57	43
Livingston	1850	332	63	37
	1860	294	74	26

TABLE XXVI

SIZES OF HOLDINGS

Eastern Piney Woods and Prairie (Washington Parish) 1860

Acres owned	Slaveholding landowners 168 — Percentage of owners	Nonslaveholding landowners 197 — Percentage of owners
1–49	3.85	21.23
50–99	6.15	15.54
100–199	10.38	24.28
200–299	6.92	14.45
300–399	13.85	7.66
400–499	9.62	3.50
500–999	33.08	9.19
1,000–4,999	15.00	.66
Above 5,000	.38	—
Not determined	.76	3.50

TABLE XXVII

SIZES OF HOLDINGS

Western Piney Woods and Prairie
(Calcasieu and Sabine Parishes) 1860

Acres owned	Slaveholding landowners 274 Percentage of owners	Nonslaveholding landowners 131 Percentage of owners
1–49	14.48	51.33
50–99	16.16	16.29
100–199	20.88	14.58
200–299	10.77	7.58
300–399	11.11	2.27
400–499	3.38	1.14
500–999	14.14	1.52
1,000–4,999	6.38	1.70
Not determined	2.37	3.60

both resembled the Alabama pine belt of 1850 in this respect. The piney woods and prairies of southwest Louisiana, however, were ten years behind the east Louisiana and southeast Mississippi region and nearly twenty years behind that of Alabama in the development of landownership. This difference from east to west in the structure of landownership indicates very clearly that agriculture was pressing upon the heels of the retreating pastoral economy and forcing the grazier to settle down as a farmer or to keep moving to more thinly populated regions.

Like those in the pine belt of the other states the slaveowners of the Louisiana piney woods and prairies possessed relatively few slaves. Washington Parish as revealed in

Table XXVIII [4] is typical of the piney woods. About forty-five of the farmers of this parish were slaveholders in 1850 and forty in 1860.

TABLE XXVIII

SLAVEHOLDING

WASHINGTON PARISH 1860	SLAVEHOLDERS 40
Slaves owned	Percentage of owners
1–4	48.09
5–9	24.59
10–19	19.13
20–29	3.83
30–39	2.19
40–49	.55
50–99	1.64

THE AGRICULTURAL ZONE

The agricultural lands, as we have previously suggested, were of uneven fertility; and nearly every county contained soils ranging from sand beds to rich, clay loams, black prairies, and alluvial soils. It is, nevertheless, possible to make a rough classification of the arable regions into the uplands and the black belt.

THE GEORGIA BLACK BELT

In Georgia the area above the pine region, continuing above the fall line into the Piedmont, and the narrow tide-water strip along the Atlantic Coast constituted the black belt. Above this are the piedmont and mountain counties.

[4] *Ibid.*, 384, for data.

All except the mountainous areas were devoted primarily to agriculture; but the black belt with the richer soils was, of course, the most productive and wealthy, both collectively and individually. Because of the fact that considerable gaps have been created in the records by the loss of numerous census returns, we have not had a free choice of counties for the purpose of analyzing the structure of land and slave ownership. Glyn on the coast, Houston, Harris, Greene, Heard, Elbert, and Henry in the interior were used as representative black-belt counties in Table XXIX.

TABLE XXIX

LANDOWNERSHIP OF THE AGRICULTURAL POPULATION

County	Year	Heads of families engaged in agriculture	Percentage of landowners	Percentage of landless
Glyn	1850	121	77.69	22.31
	1860	109	84.40	15.60
Harris	1850	1,063	78.08	21.92
	1860	934	74.84	25.16
Greene	1850	633	76.30	23.70
	1860	474	83.54	16.46
Heard	1850	614	68.73	31.27
	1860	674	69.73	30.27
Houston	1850	970	74.63	25.44
	1860	721	78.92	21.08
Elbert	1850	997	71.41	28.59
	(1860 Census lost)			
Henry	1850	1,471	73.83	26.17
	(1860 Census lost)			

Tables XXX and XXXI give the landownership of the slaveholders and nonslaveholders separately for the Georgia black belt.

TABLE XXX

LANDOWNERSHIP OF THE SLAVEHOLDING FARMERS

County	Year	Heads of families engaged in agriculture	Percentage of landowners	Percentage of landless
Glyn	1850	85	90.59	9.41
	1860	64	95.31	4.69
Harris	1850	661	92.58	7.42
	1860	524	89.50	10.50
Greene	1850	473	91.12	8.88
	1860	359	93.59	6.41
Heard	1850	263	87.07	12.93
	1860	272	89.71	10.29
Houston	1850	592	91.05	8.95
	1860	465	91.18	8.82
Elbert	1850	475	90.53	9.47
	(1860 Census lost)			
Henry	1850	669	92.83	7.17
	(1860 Census lost)			

From these tables it will be observed that in 1850 about 50 per cent of the nonslaveholders and about 91 per cent of the slaveholders owned their farms in the black belt; that ten years later approximately 58 per cent of the non-slaveholders and 92 per cent of the slaveholders were land-owners. It is significant that the greatest increase in landownership of the nonslaveholders occurred in two of the older counties, Glyn and Greene. The explanation seems to lie in the great amounts of land sold for taxes or at frontier prices because of the exodus from the older counties into southwest Georgia or farther west. Indeed, as we have observed, the competition of the cheaper and fresher lands to the west cheapened the lands on the seaboard states so that those who did not wish to leave the old community had a better chance to become landowners.

TABLE XXXI

LANDOWNERSHIP OF THE NONSLAVEHOLDING FARMERS

County	Year	Heads of families engaged in agriculture	Percentage of landowners	Percentage of landless
Glyn	1850	36	47.22	52.78
	1860	45	68.89	31.11
Harris	1850	402	54.23	45.77
	1860	410	56.10	43.90
Greene	1850	160	32.50	67.50
	1860	115	52.17	47.83
Heard	1850	351	54.99	45.01
	1860	402	56.22	43.78
Houston	1850	378	48.94	51.05
	1860	256	56.64	43.36
Elbert	1850	522	54.02	45.98
	(1860 Census lost)			
Henry	1850	802	57.98	42.02
	(1860 Census lost)			

Tables XXXII and XXXIII analyze the sizes of holdings of both the slaveholding and nonslaveholding farmers for 1850 and 1860 in the seven black-belt counties together and in one sample county.

TABLE XXXII

Sizes of Holdings

	GEORGIA BLACK BELT AS A WHOLE, 1850		HOUSTON COUNTY 1850	
	Slave-holding landowners 2,939	Nonslave-holding landowners 1,412	Slave-holding landowners 539	Nonslave-holding landowners 185
Acres owned	Percentage of owners	Percentage of owners	Percentage of owners	Percentage of owners
1–50	2.55	14.16	2.04	17.29
51–100	8.61	28.97	6.30	25.94
101–200	19.73	31.16	15.95	35.67
201–300	17.90	14.87	16.32	11.35
301–400	12.62	4.82	17.25	7.02
401–500	9.32	2.48	8.90	1.08
501–1,000	19.72	2.62	20.96	1.62
1,001–5,000	9.12	.21	11.69	—
Above 5,000	.24	—	.56	—

From these tables it can be seen at a glance that in the black belt of Georgia the bulk of landowners, both slaveholders and nonslaveholders, engaged in agriculture possessed from 1 to 500 acres of land. In 1850, 70 per cent of the slaveholders and 96 per cent of the nonslaveholders owned less than 500 acres, while in 1860, 56 per cent of the slaveholders and 96 per cent of the nonslaveholders who owned land fell in the 1-to-500-acre category.

The analysis of landownership would seem to indicate that the bulk of slaveholders in the Georgia black belt, like the nonslaveholders, were farmers rather than planters. An

TABLE XXXIII

SIZES OF HOLDINGS

	GEORGIA BLACK BELT * AS A WHOLE, 1860		HOUSTON COUNTY 1860	
	Slave-holding landowners 1,534	Nonslave-holding landowners 692	Slave-holding landowners 424	Nonslave-holding landowners 145
Acres owned	Percentage of owners	Percentage of owners	Percentage of owners	Percentage of owners
1–50	2.15	12.57	.47	11.71
51–100	5.22	29.20	5.43	26.21
101–200	14.60	35.12	8.02	27.59
201–300	15.52	11.13	16.51	17.24
301–400	11.73	5.92	12.50	9.66
401–500	7.11	2.31	5.19	2.07
501–1,000	24.64	2.46	24.06	2.76
1,001–5,000	18.25	1.29	27.59	2.76
Above 5,000	.78	—	.24	—

* Only Greene, Glyn, Houston, Harris, and Heard counties are used in this table for 1860, since Schedule IV for Henry and Elbert counties could not be found when the statistical data for the above tabulation were being assembled.

analysis of slaveholding proves this to be true. Slaveholding in Houston County for 1850 and 1860 as given in Table XXXIV may be considered typical of the whole region.

TABLE XXXIV

SLAVEHOLDING

Houston County

Slaves owned	1850 Slaveholders 592 Percentage of owners	1860 Slaveholders 465 Percentage of owners
1–5	35.97	27.74
6–10	19.25	20.22
11–20	18.75	18.28
21–30	11.65	9.68
31–40	6.25	9.25
41–50	2.87	4.52
51–100	4.55	8.39
101–500	.67	1.73

THE GEORGIA UPLANDS

The counties in the Georgia piedmont that have been selected as representative of that region are Floyd, Forsyth, Franklin, Gordon, and Hall. The soil in these counties was usually very good; but much of the county was broken, even mountainous in places, and easily eroded when put under cultivation. It is really a transitional zone between the old Georgia black belt, which lay above the fall line, and the mountains to the north. The bulk of the farming was carried on in the valleys and lower hills, while the grazing of livestock was the principal occupation of those who inhabited the more broken portions of the Piedmont. The ownership of land in the rougher portions where grazing was the chief business was not of prime importance as long as the country was sparsely settled and the ranges were open.

Table XXXV shows the distribution of landownership of the agricultural population in 1850 and 1860.

TABLE XXXV

LANDOWNERSHIP OF THE AGRICULTURAL POPULATION

County	Year	Heads of families engaged in agriculture	Percentage of landowners	Percentage of landless
Floyd	1850	674	63.50	36.50
	1860	1,206	63.52	36.48
Forsyth	1850	1,210	69.09	30.91
	1860	1,074	66.95	33.05
Franklin	1850	1,492	77.35	22.65
	1860	941	54.41	45.59
Gordon	1850	678	52.51	47.49
	1860	1,045	59.43	40.57
Hall	1850	1,079	68.95	31.05
	1860	1,121	66.90	33.10

About 66 per cent of those engaged in agriculture owned their farms in 1850 and 62 per cent in 1860. This pattern of ownership is more like that of the mountains for this period or the pine belt in the Southwest.

Tables XXXVI and XXXVII divide the landowners into slaveholders and nonslaveholders.

In 1850 approximately 59 per cent of the nonslaveholders were landowners, and in 1860 about 54 per cent owned their land. Over 90 per cent of the slaveholders owned their land in 1850 and 1860. The decline in the percentage of landownership of the nonslaveholders was probably due to

TABLE XXXVI

LANDOWNERSHIP OF THE SLAVEHOLDING FARMERS

County	Year	Heads of families engaged in agriculture	Percentage of landowners	Percentage of landless
Floyd	1850	202	91.58	8.42
	1860	404	92.82	7.18
Forsyth	1850	194	95.36	4.64
	1860	157	96.18	3.82
Franklin	1850	383	98.69	1.31
	1860	198	83.84	16.16
Gordon	1850	121	86.78	13.22
	1860	237	94.94	5.06
Hall	1850	195	93.33	6.67
	1860	197	97.46	2.54

TABLE XXXVII

LANDOWNERSHIP OF THE NONSLAVEHOLDING FARMERS

County	Year	Heads of families engaged in agriculture	Percentage of landowners	Percentage of landless
Floyd	1850	472	51.48	48.52
	1860	802	48.75	51.25
Forsyth	1850	1,016	64.08	35.92
	1860	917	61.94	38.06
Franklin	1850	1,109	69.97	30.03
	1860	743	46.57	53.43
Gordon	1850	557	45.06	54.94
	1860	808	49.01	50.99
Hall	1850	884	63.57	34.43
	1860	924	60.39	39.61

the migration of large numbers of nonslaveholding land-owners to the Southwest. Tables XXXVIII and XXXIX for 1850 and 1860 analyze the sizes of holdings of both slave-holders and nonslaveholders in the region as a whole and in a typical county.

TABLE XXXVIII

SIZES OF HOLDINGS

	GEORGIA UPLANDS AS A WHOLE, 1850		HALL COUNTY 1850	
	Slave-holding landowners 1,035	Nonslave-holding landowners 2,483	Slave-holding landowners 182	Nonslave-holding landowners 562
Acres owned	Percentage of owners	Percentage of owners	Percentage of owners	Percentage of owners
1–50	2.80	17.04	2.75	7.12
51–100	6.48	20.86	2.75	16.73
101–200	20.48	32.70	12.64	33.63
201–300	14.69	14.38	13.19	24.91
301–400	14.98	7.21	14.29	8.19
401–500	10.72	3.14	13.19	4.45
501–1,000	20.19	3.83	28.57	4.63
1,001–5,000	9.37	.84	12.09	.36
Above 5,000	.29	—	.55	—

Of the slaveholders 70 per cent in 1850 and 72 per cent in 1860 owned from 1 to 500 acres and would be generally classed as farmers, while 95 and 96 per cent of the nonslaveholders were in this class of landholders at those respective times.

TABLE XXXIX

SIZES OF HOLDINGS

	GEORGIA UPLANDS AS A WHOLE, 1860		HALL COUNTY 1860	
	Slaveholding landowners 1,109	Nonslaveholding landowners 2,259	Slaveholding landowners 192	Nonslaveholding landowners 558
Acres owned	Percentage of owners	Percentage of owners	Percentage of owners	Percentage of owners
1–50	1.35	11.95	.52	11.83
51–100	4.60	21.43	2.60	17.38
101–200	23.45	36.43	16.15	24.55
201–300	16.32	15.80	22.40	25.63
301–400	16.86	7.66	11.46	8.78
401–500	9.74	3.19	10.94	5.91
501–1,000	19.66	2.97	26.56	5.02
1,001–5,000	7.84	.57	9.37	—
Above 5,000	.18	.09	—	—

Table XL shows the distribution of slaveholdings in Hall County, which was fairly typical of the Georgia uplands.

TABLE XL

SLAVEHOLDING

Hall County

Slaves owned	1850 Slaveholders 195 Percentage of owners	1860 Slaveholders 197 Percentage of owners
1–5	63.08	67.52
6–10	20.00	20.81
11–20	12.31	9.65
21–30	3.59	1.02
31–40	1.03	.51
41–50	—	.51

THE ALABAMA BLACK BELT

While the prairie region of upper south Alabama is spoken of as the Alabama "black belt," the valley lands of north Alabama, especially those of the Tennessee and Coosa valleys, were economically and socially a portion of the black belt. In analyzing the landownership of the black belt, only counties from the prairie region have been chosen because of the fact that the agricultural schedule (IV) for the rich-land counties of the Tennessee Valley could not be located when this study was being made. However, the less fertile Tennessee Valley counties of Lauderdale and Lawrence will be treated to some extent in connection with the agricultural hill counties.

Table XLI gives an analysis of the distribution of land-ownership in the black belt. First the landownership of both slaveholding and nonslaveholding operators is analyzed, and then the operators are separated into slaveholders and nonslaveholders. About 60 per cent of the agricultural population of the black belt were slaveholders and 40 per cent were nonslaveholders.

TABLE XLI

LANDOWNERSHIP OF THE AGRICULTURAL POPULATION

County	Year	Heads of families engaged in agriculture	Percentage of landowners	Percentage of landless
Dallas *	1850	590 (about)	82.00	18.00
	1860	570	84.04	15.96
Greene †	1837	600	52.70	47.30
	1844	900 (about)	60.37	39.63
	1856	1,000 (about)	81.95	18.05
	1860	889	82.09	17.91
Lowndes	1850	1,155	79.74	20.26
	1860	1,147	76.63	23.37
Marengo	1850	1,002	75.25	24.75
	1860	770	86.75	13.25
Monroe	1850	819	68.50	31.50
	1860	840	83.57	16.43
Montgomery	1850	1,071	72.00	28.00
	1860	1,008	76.09	23.91
Perry	1850	1,192	83.56	16.44
	1860	1,003	78.96	21.04

* Schedule IV for Dallas County in 1850 is missing, and the analysis of landownership for that date was based on the tax books.

† Schedule IV for Greene was lost when these statistics were prepared, and the tax books, in the county courthouse at Eutaw, for 1837, 1844, and 1856, together with the census Schedules I and II for that county, were used as substitutes for Schedule IV.

TABLE XLII

LANDOWNERSHIP OF THE SLAVEHOLDING FARMERS

County	Year	Heads of families engaged in agriculture	Percentage of landowners	Percentage of landless
Dallas	1850	(data incomplete)		
	1860	494	89.27	10.73
Greene	1837 1844 1856	(data incomplete)		
	1860	720	88.47	11.53
Lowndes	1850	714	89.92	10.08
	1860	693	89.74	11.26
Marengo	1850	702	90.17	9.83
	1860	549	90.50	9.50
Monroe	1850	437	84.67	15.33
	1860	417	93.53	6.47
Montgomery	1850	597	85.09	14.91
	1860	638	91.22	8.78
Perry	1850	743	95.02	4.98
	1860	501	89.42	10.58

Tables XLI, XLII, and XLIII show that the percentage of landowners had increased in Dallas, Greene, Marengo, Monroe, and Montgomery and had decreased slightly in Lowndes and Perry. In separating the nonslaveholders from the slaveholders it appears that the percentage of nonslaveholding landowners increased in Marengo, Monroe, and Perry and decreased in Lowndes and Montgomery. The census data for Dallas and Greene were incomplete; but the tax lists for Greene show that 20 per cent of the nonslave-

TABLE XLIII

LANDOWNERSHIP OF THE NONSLAVEHOLDING FARMERS

County	Year	Heads of families engaged in agriculture	Percentage of landowners	Percentage of landless
Dallas	1850	(data incomplete)		
	1860	76	50.00	50.00
Greene	1837			
	1844	(data incomplete)		
	1856			
	1860	179	56.42	43.58
Lowndes	1850	441	63.27	36.73
	1860	454	58.15	41.85
Marengo	1850	300	40.33	59.67
	1860	221	77.38	22.62
Monroe	1850	382	50.00	50.00
	1860	423	73.76	26.24
Montgomery	1850	474	54.85	45.15
	1860	370	50.00	50.00
Perry	1850	449	64.59	35.41
	1860	502	68.58	31.47

holders of all vocations—the tax books do not indicate a person's profession—owned farm land in 1837, about 34 per cent in 1844, and 74 per cent in 1856. In Dallas County where only a small number of nonslaveholders were engaged in agriculture—the bulk of this group lived in Selma and were engaged in other occupations—the data obtainable at the time this material was collected was insufficient for a complete analysis of the agricultural population. While the percentage of landowners in Dallas increased from 82 to 84 per cent, it cannot, however, be determined whether or not both slaveholders and nonslaveholders shared in this increase.

In the black belt, the number of slaveholders who were listed as owners, remained practically stationary at just above an average of 90 per cent. It must be said, however, at this point that practically all of the 10 per cent landless slaveholding farmers in Alabama and elsewhere were sons, sons-in-law, or near relatives of the owners of farms and plantations, and were usually cultivating land which belonged to their families and which they would eventually possess. The same observation usually applies to the non-slaveholder who owned more land than he and his minor

TABLE XLIV

SIZES OF HOLDINGS

	ALABAMA BLACK BELT AS A WHOLE, 1850		PERRY COUNTY 1850	
	Slave-holding landowners 2,351	Nonslave-holding landowners 881	Slave-holding landowners 706	Nonslave-holding landowners 290
Acres owned	Percentage of owners	Percentage of owners	Percentage of owners	Percentage of owners
1–50	4.38	27.47	3.54	27.93
51–100	7.53	24.29	8.50	23.79
101–200	20.20	28.04	22.38	28.97
201–300	13.57	6.92	15.16	7.59
301–400	12.17	4.20	12.89	4.14
401–500	7.19	2.04	6.80	1.38
501–1,000	20.54	2.27	19.12	2.07
1,001–5,000	13.14	—	10.62	—
Above 5,000	.30	—	—	—
Not determined	.98	4.77	.99	4.13

children could cultivate. This relationship is apparent in the juxtaposition of family names in the agricultural schedule (IV) and it is occasionally referred to in wills.

An analysis of the sizes of the landholdings of these two classes indicates a pattern of ownership strikingly similar to that of the Georgia black belt. Table XLIV is an analysis of the black belt based on the counties of Marengo, Monroe, Lowndes, and Perry for which the records of 1850 are complete. Perry County follows this composite picture very closely and will serve as a specific illustration of the structure of ownership of the nonslaveholders in this area.[5]

As previously explained, the agricultural schedule for 1860 could not be found when this material was assembled and the analysis was based upon the census of 1850. Several tax books have been examined, however, including those of Lawrence County for 1862, Greene for 1856, and Montgomery for 1858, and, while there was no fundamental change, the same trend may be observed as in the black belt of Georgia—indeed even as in the Pine Belt of all the states—namely a considerable increase among both slaveholders and nonslaveholders of those owning from one hundred to four hundred acres. In 1850 approximately 65 per cent of the slaveholding landowners and 93 per cent of the nonslaveholding landowners in the sample counties possessed between 1 and 500 acres of land, while 46 per cent of the slaveholders and 39 per cent of the nonslaveholders owned between 100 and 400 acres. As in Georgia, the bulk of the nonslaveholders and about half of the slaveholders who owned land fell in the same land category of medium-

---

[5] The figures here differ slightly from those in Frank L. and Harriet C. Owsley, "The Economic Basis of Society in the Late ante-Bellum South" in *Journal of Southern History*, IV (1940), 39, because Bibb County was not included. This article gives more detailed information than is possible here.

sized to large farmer. An analysis of slaveholding supports this conclusion. Perry will be used as a representative black-belt county. The records of slaveholding for 1850 and 1860 are complete and both years will be used in Table XLV.

TABLE XLV

SLAVEHOLDING

Perry County

Slaves owned	1850 Slaveholders 743 Percentage of owners	1860 Slaveholders 501 Percentage of owners
1–5	35.26	31.74
6–10	15.61	14.06
11–20	18.98	17.00
21–30	8.61	11.34
31–40	5.65	6.00
41–50	3.63	3.39
51–100	6.59	11.87
101–200	.81	2.60
Not determined	4.85	2.00

According to this analysis about 70 per cent of the slave-holders in 1850 and 63 per cent in 1860 had from 1 to 20 slaves; and 51 per cent in 1850 and 46 per cent in 1860 owned from 1 to 10. There were few small planters among those of the first class and perhaps none at all in that group that possessed from 1 to 10 slaves.[6] By correlating the own-

[6] Occasionally, of course, one finds a small slaveholder or a nonslave-holder who owned a large plantation and employed hired slaves and free Negroes.

ership of land and slaves it is found that those who held from 1 to 10 slaves usually owned from 100 to 400 acres of land—improved and unimproved.

THE ALABAMA UPLANDS

In the uplands above the black belt, five counties have been used as representative of the area in which they lie. These are Bibb and Coosa, whose lower portions lay in the edge of the black belt, and whose soils of sand and clay loam were quite productive; Randolph and Fayette, rugged but possessed of good soils, further north nearly opposite one another on the eastern and western borders of the state respectively; and Lauderdale at the northwestern corner of the state lying in the Tennessee Valley, but having little alluvial soil comparable with the rich counties of Madison and Limestone—the latter being identical with the black belt. All of these counties had good clay and sandy loam soils, and they contained many small river and creek valleys of alluvial soil; but their general fertility was not comparable with that of the prairies and the finer clays of the black belt, and the hilly nature of the country caused rapid soil erosion. But in the late antebellum period these counties produced profitably almost any kind of field crop. The zone in which Coosa and Bibb lie had a population of farmers and small to moderate-sized planters, while Fayette and Randolph were typical "up country" counties similar to the Georgia and Carolina back country. Lauderdale was similar in many respects to Bibb and Coosa.

An analysis of the distribution and structure of the ownership of land and slaves is presented in Tables XLVI, XLVII, and XLVIII.

TABLE XLVI

LANDOWNERSHIP OF THE AGRICULTURAL POPULATION

County	Year	Heads of families engaged in agriculture	Percentage of landowners	Percentage of landless
Bibb	1850	995	68.84	31.36
	1860	1,074	69.55	30.45
Coosa	1850	1,466	74.82	25.18
	1860	1,718	78.70	21.30
Fayette *	1850	645	66.05	33.95
	1860	1,653	82.46	17.54
Lauderdale	1850	614	87.62	12.36
	1860	1,065	66.29	33.71
Randolph	1850	1,628	64.43	35.57
	1860	2,468	75.57	24.43

* A portion of Schedule IV for Fayette and Lauderdale counties was missing when these tables were made.

TABLE XLVII

LANDOWNERSHIP OF THE SLAVEHOLDING FARMERS

County	Year	Heads of families engaged in agriculture	Percentage of landowners	Percentage of landless
Bibb	1850	336	94.64	5.36
	1860	323	91.95	8.05
Coosa	1850	471	91.72	8.28
	1860	448	94.20	5.80
Fayette	1850	148	93.92	6.08
	1860	243	95.88	4.12
Lauderdale	1850	178	94.94	5.06
	1860	248	93.15	6.85
Randolph	1850	217	96.31	3.69
	1860	300	93.33	6.67

TABLE XLVIII

LANDOWNERSHIP OF THE NONSLAVEHOLDING FARMERS

County	Year	Heads of families engaged in agriculture	Percentage of landowners	Percentage of landless
Bibb	1850	659	55.39	44.61
	1860	751	59.92	40.08
Coosa	1850	995	66.83	33.17
	1860	1,270	73.23	27.17
Fayette	1850	493	57.75	42.25
	1860	1,410	80.14	19.86
Lauderdale	1850	436	84.63	15.37
	1860	817	58.14	41.86
Randolph	1850	1,411	59.53	40.47
	1860	2,168	73.11	26.89

In 1850 about 65 per cent of the nonslaveholders engaged in agriculture, and in 1860 nearly 69 per cent were landowners. The percentage of slaveholders who owned land decreased from 94.30 in 1850 to 93.70 in 1860. It will be observed that the spread of landownership in the Alabama upcountry corresponds closely to that of the Georgia piedmont.

An analysis of the sizes of holdings of the upcountry reveals a pattern of ownership similar to that of the black belt. The chief difference—and that was not as great as might be expected—was that the percentage of large holdings was greater in the black belt. Table XLIX is an analysis of the sizes of land holdings in 1850 (the agricultural schedules for 1860 could not be found, as previously explained).

TABLE XLIX

SIZES OF HOLDINGS

	ALABAMA UPLANDS AS A WHOLE, 1850		COOSA COUNTY 1850	
	Slave-holding landowners 1,267	Nonslave-holding landowners 2,526	Slave-holding landowners 432	Nonslave-holding landowners 665
Acres owned	Percentage of owners	Percentage of owners	Percentage of owners	Percentage of owners
1–50	4.26	26.80	3.70	21.35
51–100	11.21	24.19	8.80	24.96
101–200	26.28	25.14	28.70	24.06
201–300	13.97	5.27	9.72	3.61
301–400	16.50	4.24	22.22	8.12
401–500	5.92	1.03	3.94	1.05
501–1,000	14.29	1.03	13.19	.60
1,001–5,000	4.18	.04	4.17	—
Above 5,000	.16	—	—	—
Not determined	3.23	12.26	5.56	16.24

Not counting the large group, classed as "not determined," the value but not the acreage of whose real estate was given, it is found that in 1850 about 78 per cent of the slaveowners and 87 per cent of the nonslaveowners had holdings of from 1 to 500 acres, and that about 57 per cent of the slaveowners and 35 per cent of the nonslaveowners had 101 to 400 acres. An examination of the valuation of the real estate whose acreage was not determined indicates clearly that practically all of the farms of undetermined size—of both slaveholders and nonslaveholders—were under 200 acres, thus increasing the percentage of those in the several groups owning less than this amount.

Coosa and Randolph counties represent, respectively, the

TABLE L

SLAVEHOLDING

Coosa County

Slaves owned	1850 Slaveholders 471 Percentage of owners	1860 Slaveholders 448 Percentage of owners
1–5	47.35	50.89
6–10	21.66	22.77
11–20	12.95	15.18
21–30	4.67	6.03
31–40	.85	1.56
41–50	.64	1.12
51–100	1.48	1.33
101–150	.21	.67
Not determined	9.20	.45

TABLE LI

RANDOLPH COUNTY

Slaves owned	1850 Slaveholders 217 Percentage of owners	1860 Slaveholders 300 Percentage of owners
1–5	71.43	68.33
6–10	16.59	20.00
11–20	7.83	9.00
21–30	.46	1.67
31–40	—	1.00
41–50	—	—
51–100	—	—
101–150	—	—
Not determined	3.69	—

transitional zone above the black belt and the typical, iso-
lated, hill country; and an analysis of slaveownership in
both counties will be given in Tables L and LI.

In both Coosa and Randolph a large majority of slaveholders owned less than ten slaves, and in Randolph over
two thirds of the slaveowners had less than five. In Coosa,
however, there were several large plantations on the
Tallapoosa and Coosa rivers where the county extended
into the black belt, whereas in Randolph there were no
large planters and only a few who owned from 20 to 40
slaves.

THE MISSISSIPPI BLACK BELT [7]

The Mississippi black belt is in reality a series of rich-
land belts: first, the alluvial or delta region lying chiefly
between the Yazoo and the Mississippi rivers and extending
southward in a narrowing strip below Vicksburg; second,
the loess or wind-deposited soil area extending in a wide
belt the length of the state just east of the delta; and third,
the black prairies which stem from the Alabama prairies
and extend into the northeastern and upper southern portion of the state. These rich land regions compose roughly
half the area of the state. However, there is another fairly
rich soil zone lying just east of the loess strip which com-
pares favorably with the black belts in the states to the
east and which was capable of sustaining a plantation
economy. Actually, only a small region in the northeastern
part of the state could be classed with the upcountry in
Alabama, Georgia, and the Carolinas.

For analyzing the ownership of land and slaves in the

[7] The analysis of landownership in the Mississippi black belt is based
on Weaver, *Mississippi Farmers*, 64, 65. Weaver's classification differs
somewhat from the one used for Georgia, Alabama, and Tennessee.

Mississippi black belt the following counties have been selected: Bolivar and Issaquena in the Mississippi-Yazoo Delta, Jefferson and Adams, partly in the flood plain of the Mississippi below Vicksburg and partly in the loess area; Hinds in the loess soil and Marshall partly in the loess belt and partly in the north-central plateau; and Lowndes lying partly in the prairies and partly in the northeast highlands.

TABLE LII

LANDOWNERSHIP OF THE AGRICULTURAL POPULATION

County	Year	Heads of families engaged in agriculture	Percentage of landowners	Percentage of landless
Adams	1850	219	82.65	17.35
	1860	234	98.70	1.30
Bolivar	1850	73	91.78	8.22
	1860	392	64.29	35.71
Hinds	1850	1,054	89.28	10.72
	1860	861	90.13	9.87
Issaquena	1850	77	97.40	2.60
	1860	95	94.74	5.26
Jefferson	1850	535	90.80	9.20
	1860	380	88.42	11.58
Lowndes	1850	823	94.17	5.83
	1860	741	92.04	7.96
Marshall	1850	1,977	86.49	13.51
	1860	1,476	81.17	18.83

TABLE LIII

LANDOWNERSHIP OF THE SLAVEHOLDING FARMERS

County	Year	Heads of families engaged in agriculture	Percentage of landowners	Percentage of landless
Adams	1850	151	88.08	11.92
	1860	210	99.52	.48
Bolivar	1850	56	100.00	—
	1860	248	88.71	11.29
Hinds	1850	814	96.31	3.69
	1860	764	92.67	7.33
Issaquena	1850	72	100.00	—
	1860	91	94.51	5.49
Jefferson	1850	299	96.66	3.34
	1860	301	97.34	2.66
Lowndes	1850	580	97.76	2.24
	1860	498	97.19	2.81
Marshall	1850	1,169	93.33	6.67
	1860	800	93.75	6.25

Although the soil areas represented by Marshall and Lowndes compare favorably with that of the black belts of the other states, the permanent fertility of much of the alluvial soils of Mississippi—and of Louisiana—and the great expense involved in draining and dyking, places them in a category quite apart from the black belt generally. It is the delta-loess areas of Mississippi, if anywhere, that the extremes of great planter and poor white should be found. In analyzing the ownership of land and slaves,[8]

[8] The analysis of the sizes of landholdings and slaveholdings in Tables

TABLE LIV

LANDOWNERSHIP OF THE NONSLAVEHOLDERS

County	Year	Heads of families engaged in agriculture	Percentage of landowners	Percentage of landless
Adams	1850	68	70.59	29.41
	1860	24	91.67	8.33
Bolivar	1850	17	64.71	35.29
	1860	144	22.22	77.78
Hinds	1850	240	65.42	34.58
	1860	97	70.10	29.90
Issaquena	1850	5	60.00	40.00
	1860	4	100.00	—
Jefferson	1850	136	77.94	22.16
	1860	79	54.43	45.57
Lowndes	1850	243	85.60	14.40
	1860	243	81.48	18.52
Marshall	1850	808	76.61	23.39
	1860	676	66.12	33.88

therefore, the counties lying in the delta-loess belts will be treated separately from Marshall, lying partly in the loess belt and partly in the north central plateau, and Lowndes, lying partly in the black prairies.

LV, LVI, LVII, LVIII, LIX, and LX is based on Weaver, *Mississippi Farmers,* Tables 10 and 11, pp. 81–82, and Table 5, p. 39, respectively.

TABLE LV

Sizes of Holdings

	MISSISSIPPI BLACK BELT DELTA-LOESS REGION, 1850		JEFFERSON COUNTY 1850	
	Slave-holding landowners 1,334	Nonslave-holding landowners 325	Slave-holding landowners 289	Nonslave-holding landowners 106
Acres owned	Percentage of owners	Percentage of owners	Percentage of owners	Percentage of owners
1–49	2.32	12.92	1.38	13.21
50–99	5.99	13.23	5.54	14.15
100–199	11.24	20.00	11.07	16.98
200–299	11.24	9.23	12.11	5.66
300–399	11.46	4.00	11.07	6.60
400–499	8.47	3.38	6.57	3.77
500–999	24.74	10.77	26.64	15.09
1,000–4,999	19.84	6.77	24.22	7.55
Above 5,000	.59	.31	—	—
Not determined	3.98	19.38	1.38	16.98

The distribution of landownership was as high in the delta-loess region as in the less fertile black-belt areas, and the sizes of holdings were not as tradition and travelers' accounts have led us to believe. In 1850 over 75 per cent of the slaveholders had less than 1,000 acres of land. Fifty

TABLE LVI

SIZES OF HOLDINGS

	MISSISSIPPI BLACK BELT DELTA-LOESS REGION, 1860		JEFFERSON COUNTY 1860	
	Slave-holding landowners 1,516	Nonslave-holding landowners 169	Slave-holding landowners 293	Nonslave-holding landowners 43
Acres owned	Percentage of owners	Percentage of owners	Percentage of owners	Percentage of owners
1–49	1.72	6.50	.34	4.65
50–99	2.44	8.28	.68	13.95
100–199	6.33	7.69	5.12	11.63
200–299	6.86	4.73	7.17	6.98
300–399	6.99	4.73	6.48	16.28
400–499	9.10	3.55	11.60	6.98
500–999	26.05	8.28	30.72	6.98
1,000–4,999	30.80	11.83	35.84	4.65
Above 5,000	1.05	.59	.68	—
Not determined	8.71	43.79	2.05	27.91

per cent owned less than 500 acres, and 34 per cent owned between 100 and 400 acres. Thirty-three per cent of the nonslaveholders' farms were from 100 to 400 acres in size. In 1860, 60 per cent of the slaveholders owned under 1,000 acres. Thirty-three per cent owned less than 500 acres, and

TABLE LVII

SIZES OF HOLDINGS

Mississippi Black Belt

North Central Plateau

	MARSHALL COUNTY 1850		MARSHALL COUNTY 1860	
	Slave-holding landowners 1,091	Nonslave-holding landowners 619	Slave-holding landowners 751	Nonslave-holding landowners 447
Acres owned	Percentage of owners	Percentage of owners	Percentage of owners	Percentage of owners
1–49	6.42	38.45	1.73	10.74
50–99	10.00	16.64	4.39	14.77
100–199	29.51	32.79	17.84	30.43
200–299	8.62	2.58	8.66	7.38
300–399	15.03	3.55	12.65	5.37
400–499	6.32	.81	7.72	2.91
500–999	16.77	.97	25.17	4.25
1,000–4,999	5.32	—	11.32	2.46
Not determined	2.02	4.20	10.52	21.70

20 per cent owned 100 to 400 acres. The large percentage of undetermined sizes of the nonslaveholders' farms makes an analysis of the sizes of their holdings worth very little. But apparently the sizes of their farms had followed the same trend of increased size as that of the slaveholders. Because of improved farm implements and methods of cultivation the trend everywhere throughout the South was in the direction of larger holdings.

TABLE LVIII

Sizes of Holdings

Mississippi Black Belt

The Black Prairies

	LOWNDES COUNTY 1850		LOWNDES COUNTY 1860	
	Slave-holding landowners 567	Nonslave-holding landowners 208	Slave-holding landowners 484	Nonslave-holding landowners 198
Acres owned	Percentage of owners	Percentage of owners	Percentage of owners	Percentage of owners
1–49	7.58	34.13	1.03	9.60
50–99	9.35	19.23	5.79	23.74
100–199	17.28	17.79	13.84	23.74
200–299	12.70	13.46	10.74	11.11
300–399	10.23	3.37	9.50	3.54
400–499	10.05	2.40	9.09	2.02
500–999	18.87	1.92	26.45	3.03
1,000–4,999	10.93	.48	20.25	2.02
Above 5,000	.88	—	—	—
Not determined	2.12	7.21	3.31	21.21

The ownership of land in Marshall and Lowndes counties was strikingly similar to that of the black belt of Alabama and Georgia, where the majority of slaveholders and the bulk of the nonslaveholders owned less than five hundred acres of land.

Table LIX, page 201, and Table LX, page 202, are an analysis of slaveholding in Jefferson and Lowndes, fairly representative of the delta-loess region and of the black-belt counties outside the alluvial soils.

TABLE LIX

SLAVEHOLDING

Jefferson County

Slaves owned	1850 Slaveholders 305 Percentage of owners	1860 Slaveholders 298 Percentage of owners
1–4	19.43	13.40
5–9	15.45	11.73
10–19	16.70	16.08
20–29	11.45	13.40
30–39	10.47	12.06
40–49	5.23	5.03
50–90	19.31	23.26
100–499	1.93	4.69
Above 500	—	.33

In the delta-loess county of Jefferson, 51 per cent of the slaveholders engaged in agriculture in 1850 owned less than 20 slaves and were not, according to the custom, classed as planters. Another 21 per cent owned from 19 to 39 slaves, which marked them as small planters. Only a fraction of the remaining 28 per cent were of the large planter class. In 1860 about 41 per cent owned less than 20 slaves and 25 per cent owned from 19 to 39. The small planter class had increased at the expense of the slaveholding farmer group. The agricultural population of the delta-loess belt was thus constituted of farmers and small planters rather than nabobs.

That part of the black belt of Mississippi represented by Lowndes had a larger proportion of farmers and small

TABLE LX

SLAVEHOLDING

Lowndes County

Slaves owned	1850 Slaveholders 580 Percentage of owners	1860 Slaveholders 498 Percentage of owners
1–4	25.53	20.70
5–9	20.19	13.70
10–19	21.91	21.00
20–29	11.88	11.65
30–39	6.55	7.85
40–49	3.45	7.65
50–99	9.62	14.45
100–499	.86	3.00

planters than did the delta-loess region as represented by Jefferson County. In 1850 those owning less than 20 slaves comprised 67 per cent of the agricultural families, whereas those having from 19 to 39 slaves made up 18 per cent. In 1860 approximately 55 per cent held fewer than 20 slaves and 19 per cent had from 19 to 39.

THE MISSISSIPPI UPLANDS

Tishomingo in the northeast corner of the state is typical in soil and topography of the upland counties in northeastern Mississippi and similar to the upland or hill counties in Georgia, Alabama, and Louisiana. The Chickasaw Indians had not been removed from this portion of Mississippi until after 1832, and there were still large tracts of public land in the region in 1850. The public domain attracted thousands of nonslaveholders and small slaveholders into this region between 1850 and 1860. Most of them became squatters under the Pre-emption Act of 1841, which permitted them after one year to acquire 160 acres at $1.25 an acre. The effect of this influx of settlers, many of whom had not perfected their land titles by 1860, reduced the percentage of landowners; it also increased the proportion of small holdings. The pattern of land and slave holding in Tishomingo follows that in the uplands of Georgia, Alabama, Louisiana, and in great portions of Tennessee.

Tables LXI, LXII, and LXIII analyze the land and slave holdings of Tishomingo County,[9] which is treated as representative of the northeastern hill region.

TABLE LXI

LANDOWNERSHIP OF THE AGRICULTURAL POPULATION

County	Year	Heads of families engaged in agriculture	Percentage of landowners	Percentage of landless
Tishomingo	1850	1,917	75.74	24.26
	1860	2,479	64.95	35.05

LANDOWNERSHIP OF THE SLAVEHOLDING FARMERS

County	Year	Heads of families engaged in agriculture	Percentage of landowners	Percentage of landless
Tishomingo	1850	300	95.67	4.33
	1860	508	91.54	8.46

[9] Based on Weaver, *Mississippi Farmers*, Table 5, p. 39, tables on pp. 65 and 70, and Tables 10 and 11, pp. 81–82.

TABLE LXI (*continued*)

LANDOWNERSHIP OF THE NONSLAVEHOLDING FARMERS

County	Year	Heads of families engaged in agriculture	Percent- age of landowners	Percent- age of landless
Tishomingo	1850	1,617	72.05	27.95
	1860	1,971	58.60	41.40

TABLE LXII

SIZES OF HOLDINGS

Mississippi Uplands

	TISHOMINGO COUNTY 1850		TISHOMINGO COUNTY 1860	
	Slave- holding landowners 287	Nonslave- holding landowners 1,165	Slave- holding landowners 455	Nonslave- holding landowners 1,155
Acres owned	Percentage of owners	Percentage of owners	Percentage of owners	Percentage of owners
1–49	2.44	1.12	2.20	4.16
50–99	2.09	11.59	4.62	14.98
100–199	31.71	49.53	23.30	44.33
200–299	6.27	6.27	10.11	9.87
300–399	20.21	10.13	14.95	8.92
400–499	11.15	3.09	13.63	3.72
500–999	16.03	3.52	16.26	3.55
1,000–4,999	6.27	—	11.43	1.13
Above 5,000	—	—	.44	—
Not determined	3.87	14.76	3.08	9.35

TABLE LXIII

SLAVEHOLDING

Tishomingo County

Slaves owned	1850 Slaveholders 300 Percentage of owners	1860 Slaveholders 508 Percentage of owners
1–4	59.16	50.54
5–9	25.02	21.12
10–19	10.32	18.76
20–29	4.26	5.80
30–39	.30	2.68
40–49	.30	.04
50–99	—	.05

LOUISIANA BLACK BELT AND UPLANDS

Harry Coles, basing his classification on Eugene W. Hilgard's study,[10] divides the agricultural lands of Louisiana into three major regions: the northern uplands, represented by Claiborne Parish; the northern alluvial, cotton-producing soils, represented by Tensas and Catahoula parishes; and the southern alluvial, sugar-producing region, represented by Ascension, West Feliciana, Iberville, and Plaquemines. In his analysis of land and slave holding in these sample parishes he finds that in 1850 and 1860 over 80 per cent of the farm operators in the southern alluvial area owned their lands. In the northern alluvial area the distribution of landownership was probably less extensive in 1850 than in the southern parishes because of the more

[10] "Physico-Geographical and Agricultural Features of the State of Louisiana," in the *Tenth Census of the United States, 1880,* 22 vols. (Washington, 1883–1885), V, 109–95.

recent settlement of the northern region. For example, although 82 per cent of the operators in Tensas Parish owned their lands, only 66 per cent in Catahoula Parish were landowners. In 1860, however, the spread of landownership in the cotton lands was greater than that of the "sugar bowl." Distribution of landownership had increased some in Tensas, but in Catahoula it had risen from 66 per cent of the agricultural population to 92 per cent.

The northern uplands represented by Claiborne Parish were being rapidly settled during the period 1850–1860. Many of the newcomers were squatters on government lands and the distribution of landownership was low. In 1850 only 68 per cent of the farmers owned their land; but

TABLE LXIV

Sizes of Holdings

Northern Alluvial Area

1860

Acres owned	Slaveholding landowners 432 Percentage of owners	Nonslaveholding landowners 421 Percentage of owners
1–49	1.85	23.52
50–59	3.00	15.20
100–199	7.87	25.18
200–299	8.33	9.26
300–399	7.63	6.41
400–499	5.09	1.18
500–999	23.84	1.66
1,000–4,999	37.50	1.18
Above 5,000	2.31	—
Not determined	2.58	16.60

by 1860 between 70 and 80 per cent had become landowners.

Tables LXIV, LXV, LXVI, and LXVII, on pages 206–209, analyzing the sizes of landholdings and slaveholdings with slight additional data derived from the text of Coles's study, are reproduced from his work.[11]

TABLE LXV

SIZES OF HOLDINGS

Southern Alluvial Area

1860

Acres owned	Slaveholding landowners 597 Percentage of owners	Nonslaveholding landowners 249 Percentage of owners
1–49	10.89	22.73
50–99	6.20	21.49
100–199	15.08	33.06
200–299	6.36	4.96
300–399	5.86	2.48
400–499	5.19	5.37
500–999	16.42	4.55
1,000–4,999	30.15	2.48
Above 5,000	3.02	—
Not determined	.84	2.89

It will be observed from these tables that the pattern of landownership of the nonslaveholders was similar to that in the agricultural zones in the other states examined. The pattern of landownership of the slaveholders was, however,

[11] Tables in *Journal of Southern History*, IX (1943), pp. 388, 389, and 390 for analysis of landholdings, and table on p. 384 for slaveholdings.

TABLE LXVI

SIZES OF HOLDINGS

Northern Oak Uplands Area (Claiborne)

1860

Acres owned	Slaveholding landowners 561 Percentage of owners	Nonslaveholding landowners 653 Percentage of owners
1–49	1.65	7.95
50–99	2.97	10.98
100–199	9.57	29.17
200–299	12.54	19.89
300–399	14.03	11.74
400–499	13.37	6.25
500–999	29.21	7.95
1,000–4,999	15.68	1.14
Above 5,000	.16	—
Not determined	.83	4.92

different from that of the same group in all areas examined except the delta-loess regions of Mississippi, where plantations above 1,000 acres in size were numerous. Indeed the percentage of plantations above 1,000 acres in Louisiana was greater than in Mississippi. The same observation with reference to slaveholding may be made in the cotton-producing region. Although in the other alluvial and prairie regions the pattern was similar to that in the other states, here nearly 60 per cent owned more than 50 slaves in 1860.

TABLE LXVII

SLAVEHOLDING 1860

Slaves owned	Tensas Cotton-producing region 187 Percentage of owners	Ascension Sugar-producing region 145 Percentage of owners	Claiborne Diversified agriculture 618 Percentage of owners
1–4	1.09	33.80	34.69
5–9	3.83	19.01	23.29
10–19	7.66	14.08	24.92
20–29	10.93	6.34	8.96
30–39	9.29	2.11	4.40
40–49	8.74	3.52	2.44
50–99	31.69	8.45	1.30
100–499	25.69	11.27	—
Above 500	1.09	1.41	—

TENNESSEE [12]

The state of Tennessee has been selected as fairly representative of the upper middle South. Its eastern and central portions are separated from the lower South by a low extension of the Applachian Mountains, while the western portion is an extension of Mississippi and Alabama and belongs economically and socially in the cotton belt.

In view of the tradition that Tennessee was essentially a state of landowning farmers, with an occasional large planter in Middle and West Tennessee, it may be surprising

[12] For a more detailed treatment of Tennessee, see Blanche Henry Clarke [Mrs. Herbert Weaver], *Tennessee Yeomen, 1850–1860,* (Nashville, 1942); Frank L. and Harriet C. Owsley, "The Economic Structure of Rural Tennessee, 1850–1860," in *Journal of Southern History,* VIII (1942), 162–82; and Chase Mooney, "Some Institutional and Statistical Aspects of Slavery in Tennessee," *Tennessee Historical Quarterly,* I (1942), 197–228.

to discover that the ownership of land was not so well distributed as in the lower South. Nor were there as many landowners in proportion to the population in East Tennessee as in Middle and West Tennessee. Moreover, a smaller proportion of nonslaveholders owned land in East Tennessee than in Middle and West Tennessee, and a smaller proportion in Tennessee as a whole than in the lower South. This is due, no doubt, to the fact that both East Tennessee and Middle Tennessee, including the bluegrass basin, contains a large proportion of rugged hills and ridges fitted only for grazing and timber. This intermingling of rich valley and ridge land makes impossible, except in the case of a few counties in the high mountains, the task of segregating the strictly agricultural counties from those predominantly devoted to grazing the open range. Actually some of the East Tennessee counties, through which the Great Valley and its tributaries pass, were rich agricultural regions even though there were towering mountains on each side. On the other hand some of the Middle Tennessee counties on the very edge of the bluegrass basin were so rugged that they were devoted primarily to grazing livestock. Tennessee will, therefore, be dealt with as a separate problem.

Eighteen counties have been selected from the three major political and geographical divisions of the state—East, Middle, and West Tennessee. Counties were selected in these larger divisions with reference to soil and topography. In East Tennessee, Grainger, Greene, Hawkins, and Johnson were chosen as representative of that region. Greene has fewer mountains and much rich valley land with clay and lime soil; Johnson occupies the other extreme with numerous ranges of hills and mountains fitted for timber and grazing, but less valley land; Hawkins and

Grainger occupy a middle ground. Middle Tennessee was divided into the bluegrass basin and the highland rim, though some of the highland rim counties chosen extend into the central or bluegrass basin. The following counties were selected from the highland rim: DeKalb and Fentress along the east and northeast of the rim, with thin shale soil lacking in lime and phosphate; Franklin and Lincoln toward the southeast of the rim, lying partly in the bluegrass basin, with soil varying from rich lime clay to shale; Montgomery and Robertson on the northern rim, whose surface is gently rolling tableland and whose soil has much clay and lime content. In the bluegrass basin, Davidson, Maury, Wilson, and Sumner, the soil of which has much clay, lime, and phosphate, were used as representative counties. In West Tennessee, Dyer, Fayette, Gibson, and Haywood, lying partly within the old coastal plain, with soils of clay loam, silt, and lime, were selected as representative counties.

Table LXVIII, calculated upon the basis of the heads of agricultural families of the sample East Tennessee counties, is a picture for that region of the distribution of landownership in 1850 and 1860.

In Greene and Grainger there was an increase in the percentage of landownership; but in Hawkins and Johnson there was a decrease. In all these counties a majority of the heads of agricultural families—about 60 per cent in 1850 and 1860—owned their farms, but not so large a proportion as in Middle and West Tennessee and in the lower South. Landownership outside of the fertile valleys, as frequently pointed out, was not of paramount importance in these highland counties; for in the mountains and coves the people were engaged primarily in grazing livestock—particularly swine—upon the open range where the nuts

TABLE LXVIII

EAST TENNESSEE

Landownership of the Agricultural Population

County	Year	Heads of families engaged in agriculture	Percent- age of landowners	Percent- age of landless
Grainger	1850	1,398	53.29	46.71
	1860	1,238	57.11	42.89
Greene	1850	2,168	60.01	39.99
	1860	2,557	64.45	35.55
Hawkins	1850	1,497	62.39	37.61
	1860	1,614	54.89	45.11
Johnson	1850	471	68.37	31.63
	1860	692	62.86	37.14

TABLE LXIX

MIDDLE TENNESSEE—HIGHLAND RIM

Landownership of the Agricultural Population

County	Year	Heads of families engaged in agriculture	Percent- age of landowners	Percent- age of landless
DeKalb	1850	998	61.94	38.06
	1860	1,227	65.44	34.56
Fentress	1850	641	57.25	42.75
	1860	763	68.55	31.45
Franklin	1850	1,236	69.99	30.01
	1860	1,306	65.39	34.61
Montgomery	1850	1,548	70.67	29.33
	1860	1,242	77.70	22.30
Robertson	1850	1,587	78.70	21.30
	1860	1,563	84.96	15.04

and mast fatten them without much aid from the corn cribs.

Tables LXIX and LXX give the distribution of landownership according to heads of agricultural families, and divide Middle Tennessee, as previously stated, into the highland rim and bluegrass basin.

TABLE LXX

MIDDLE TENNESSEE—BLUEGRASS BASIN

Landownership of the Agricultural Population

County	Year	Heads of families engaged in agriculture	Percentage of landowners	Percentage of landless
Davidson	1850	1,854	62.24	37.76
	1860	1,542	65.37	34.63
Maury	1850	2,340	55.24	44.76
	1860	2,381	70.98	29.02
Sumner	1850	1,999	68.49	31.51
	1860	1,934	80.30	19.70
Wilson	1850	2,675	65.20	34.80
	1860	2,412	79.35	20.65

On the highland rim about 68 per cent of the agricultural population in 1850 and 72 in 1860 owned their land. In the bluegrass basin about 63 per cent of the agricultural population in 1850 and approximately 75 per cent in 1860 were landowners. The disposal of school lands to squatters who had occupied these lands for a number of years and the sale of unimproved land held for speculation account for the general increase in the ownership of land during the decade from 1850 to 1860.

West Tennessee was similar to the black belt in the lower South in soil and topography and was well fitted for growing cotton, grain, and hay. Despite the fact that it had been opened to settlement several decades later than Middle Tennessee, it had apparently reached about the same state of development by 1850 as the bluegrass region and the better agricultural counties of the highland rim. Here, as in the other areas examined, all categories of landowners were intermingled as shown in the agricultural schedules of the censuses of 1850 and 1860, and by the tax books.

Table LXXI (based upon the census returns) gives the distribution of landownership in West Tennessee for 1850 and 1860.

TABLE LXXI

WEST TENNESSEE

Landownership of the Agricultural Population

County	Year	Heads of families engaged in agriculture	Percent-age of landowners	Percent-age of landless
Dyer	1850	753	71.98	28.02
	1860	1,129	66.43	33.57
Fayette	1850	1,487	73.50	26.50
	1860	1,215	77.53	22.47
Gibson	1850	2,422	67.88	32.12
	1860	2,509	70.31	29.69
Haywood	1850	1,244	60.77	39.23
	1860	1,145	79.39	20.61

Thus the distribution of landownership had increased from 69 to 74 per cent between 1850 and 1860. Farm ownership in Tennessee stood about thus in 1860: in East Tennessee where grazing on the open range was generally as important as agriculture, 60 per cent of the agricultural families owned their land; on the highland rim where grazing was nearly as important, 72 per cent; in the bluegrass basin, 75 per cent; and in West Tennessee, 74 per cent. The potential ownership, as we have observed before, was considerably higher than these figures indicate if one takes into account the sons, sons-in-law, and other relatives who were using the family land free of charge, or considers the farmer or planter who lived in one county and owned land in another.

Just what portion of the slaveholders and nonslaveholders owned their lands will be seen from Tables LXXII, LXXIII, LXXIV, LXXV, LXXVI, LXXVII, LXXVIII, and LXXIX, on pages 215–19.

TABLE LXXII

East Tennessee

Landownership of the Slaveholding Farmers

County	Year	Heads of families engaged in agriculture	Percentage of landowners	Percentage of landless
Grainger	1850	165	90.50	9.50
	1860	167	96.41	3.59
Greene	1850	216	93.06	6.94
	1860	225	96.00	4.00
Hawkins	1850	260	90.38	9.62
	1860	244	93.03	6.97
Johnson	1850	47	97.87	2.13
	1860	52	84.62	15.38

TABLE LXXIII

EAST TENNESSEE

Landownership of the Nonslaveholding Farmers

County	Year	Heads of families engaged in agriculture	Percentage of landowners	Percentage of landless
Grainger	1850	1,233	48.34	51.66
	1860	1,071	50.98	49.02
Greene	1850	1,592	56.35	43.65
	1860	2,332	61.41	38.59
Hawkins	1850	1,237	56.51	43.49
	1860	1,370	48.10	51.90
Johnson	1850	426	65.09	34.91
	1860	640	61.09	38.91

TABLE LXXIV

MIDDLE TENNESSEE—HIGHLAND RIM

Landownership of the Slaveholding Farmers

County	Year	Heads of families engaged in agriculture	Percentage of landowners	Percentage of landless
DeKalb	1850	152	86.18	13.82
	1860	191	95.29	4.71
Fentress	1850	45	93.33	6.67
	1860	51	92.16	7.84
Franklin	1850	400	92.50	7.50
	1860	409	90.22	9.78
Montgomery	1850	779	88.96	11.04
	1860	638	92.48	7.52
Robertson	1850	692	94.12	5.88
	1860	640	96.72	3.28

TABLE LXXV

MIDDLE TENNESSEE—HIGHLAND RIM

Landownership of the Nonslaveholding Farmers

County	Year	Heads of families engaged in agriculture	Percentage of landowners	Percentage of landless
DeKalb	1850	836	57.54	42.26
	1860	1,036	59.94	40.06
Fentress	1850	596	54.53	45.47
	1860	712	66.85	33.15
Franklin	1850	836	59.21	40.79
	1860	897	54.07	45.93
Montgomery	1850	769	52.15	47.85
	1860	604	62.09	37.91
Robertson	1850	958	68.58	31.42
	1860	923	76.81	23.19

In round numbers 92 per cent of the slaveholders in East Tennessee were landowners in 1850 and 1860; and 56 per cent of the nonslaveholders owned their farms in 1850 and 55 per cent in 1860.

On the highland rim the percentage of nonslaveholders owning land had increased from 58 in 1850 to about 64 in 1860; and the slaveholders from 91 per cent to 93 per cent.

In the bluegrass basin 44 per cent of the nonslaveholding farmers owned their farms in 1850 and about 60 per cent in 1860; in 1850, about 86 per cent of the slaveholders and in 1860 approximately 92 per cent were landowners. The increase in the landownership of the nonslaveholders in the bluegrass basin and on the highland rim during the last ten years of antebellum period was made possible, as previ-

TABLE LXXVI

MIDDLE TENNESSEE—BLUEGRASS BASIN

Landownership of the Slaveholding Farmers

County	Year	Heads of families engaged in agriculture	Percent- age of landowners	Percent- age of landless
Davidson	1850	928	84.48	15.52
	1860	731	90.29	9.71
Maury	1850	1,043	80.82	19.18
	1860	1,130	87.26	12.74
Sumner	1850	789	92.14	7.86
	1860	707	94.63	5.37
Wilson	1850	1,066	88.46	11.54
	1860	1,027	95.13	4.87

TABLE LXXVII

MIDDLE TENNESSEE—BLUEGRASS BASIN

Landownership of the Nonslaveholding Farmers

County	Year	Heads of families engaged in agriculture	Percent- age of landowners	Percent- age of landless
Davidson	1850	926	39.96	60.04
	1860	811	42.91	57.09
Maury	1850	1,303	34.77	65.23
	1860	1,231	56.27	43.73
Sumner	1850	1,210	53.06	46.94
	1860	1,227	72.05	27.95
Wilson	1850	1,609	49.76	50.22
	1860	1,385	67.65	32.35

TABLE LXXVIII

WEST TENNESSEE

Landownership of the Slaveholding Farmers

County	Year	Heads of families engaged in agriculture	Percent- age of landowners	Percent- age of landless
Dyer	1850	215	94.42	5.58
	1860	337	91.99	8.01
Fayette	1850	979	88.76	11.24
	1860	797	91.84	8.16
Gibson	1850	601	91.01	8.99
	1860	872	90.60	9.40
Haywood	1850	610	81.97	18.03
	1860	610	93.93	6.07

TABLE LXXIX

WEST TENNESSEE

Landownership of the Nonslaveholding Farmers

County	Year	Heads of families engaged in agriculture	Percent- age of landowners	Percent- age of landless
Dyer	1850	538	63.01	36.99
	1860	792	55.56	44.44
Fayette	1850	508	44.09	55.91
	1860	418	50.24	49.76
Gibson	1850	1,821	60.24	39.76
	1860	1,637	59.50	40.50
Haywood	1850	634	40.38	59.62
	1860	535	62.80	37.20

TABLE LXXX

East Tennessee

Sizes of Holdings

	EAST TENNESSEE AS A WHOLE, 1850		GRAINGER COUNTY 1850	
	Slave-holding landowners 631	Nonslave-holding landowners 2,671	Slave-holding landowners 149	Nonslave-holding landowners 596
Acres owned	Percentage of owners	Percentage of owners	Percentage of owners	Percentage of owners
1–50	2.33	8.86	.67	2.85
51–100	7.51	17.94	5.37	13.76
101–200	22.29	32.23	22.82	30.20
201–300	15.62	15.04	16.11	13.09
301–400	12.75	7.54	16.78	7.72
401–500	10.97	3.11	8.72	2.52
501–1,000	18.58	4.09	20.13	3.86
1,001–5,000	8.50	1.26	7.38	1.17
Above 5,000	.42	—	—	—
Not determined	1.03	9.90	2.01	24.00

ously observed, by the sale of school lands and tracts of land held by speculators or farmers and planters with an excess of unimproved land.

From the tables on West Tennessee it will be noted that ownership of land in the nonslaveholding group was about 52 per cent in 1850 and 57 per cent in 1860, and that the ownership of land of the slaveholders increased from 89 per cent in 1850 to 92 per cent in 1860.

Thus we see that by 1860, 55 per cent of the nonslaveholding farmers in East Tennessee, 64 per cent on the highland rim, 60 in the bluegrass basin, and 57 per cent in West

TABLE LXXXI

EAST TENNESSEE

Sizes of Holdings

Acres owned	EAST TENNESSEE AS A WHOLE, 1860		GRAINGER COUNTY 1860	
	Slaveholding landowners 648	Nonslaveholding landowners 3,028	Slaveholding landowners 546	Nonslaveholding landowners 161
	Percentage of owners	Percentage of owners	Percentage of owners	Percentage of owners
1–50	.91	6.77	—	4.95
51–100	5.99	18.37	1.24	18.13
101–200	21.17	32.47	17.39	38.28
201–300	19.04	14.38	14.91	16.30
301–400	14.05	6.10	18.01	6.41
401–500	8.14	3.10	11.80	3.83
501–1,000	19.20	3.79	23.60	4.58
1,001–5,000	8.74	1.01	11.18	.55
Above 5,000	.48	—	.62	—
Not determined	2.28	14.01	1.25	6.95

Tennessee were landowners. Above 90 per cent of the slaveholders were landowners. In the case of both slaveholders and nonslaveholders the percentage, as was previously observed, would be higher when the near relatives, who would eventually inherit portions of land, are taken into account. Landownership of the slaveholders in Tennessee was about what it was in the other portions of the South; but that of the nonslaveholders was considerably lower than in Alabama, Mississippi, and Louisiana and ranked close to that of Georgia.

An examination of the sizes of farms of both slaveholders

TABLE LXXXII

MIDDLE TENNESSEE—HIGHLAND RIM

Sizes of Holdings

	HIGHLAND RIM AS A WHOLE, 1850		FRANKLIN COUNTY 1850	
	Slave-holding landowners 1,828	Nonslave-holding landowners 2,369	Slave-holding landowners 370	Nonslave-holding landowners 495
Acres owned	Percentage of owners	Percentage of owners	Percentage of owners	Percentage of owners
1–50	5.04	13.23	3.24	14.34
51–100	11.57	24.42	11.35	22.42
101–200	28.78	29.74	26.76	33.54
201–300	17.80	10.59	21.62	12.32
301–400	10.98	4.15	12.16	3.64
401–500	7.94	2.54	8.11	1.82
501–1,000	11.55	3.20	10.27	2.63
1,001–5,000	3.71	.96	3.24	.81
Above 5,000	.16	.04	.54	.20
Not determined	2.47	11.12	2.70	8.28

and nonslaveholders in the case of Tennessee reveals what has already been shown in the other states, namely, that a very large majority of the slaveholders were farmers rather than planters, and were in the same general economic class with the large core of nonslaveholders. Tables LXXX, LXXXI, LXXXII, LXXXIII, LXXXIV, LXXXV, LXXXVI, and LXXXVII present the landownership structure of both the nonslaveholders and slaveholders according to the regional groupings used for Tennessee.

TABLE LXXXIII

MIDDLE TENNESSEE—HIGHLAND RIM

Sizes of Holdings

| | HIGHLAND RIM AS A WHOLE, 1860 | | FRANKLIN COUNTY 1860 | |
| | Slave-holding landowners 1,807 | Nonslave-holding landowners 2,666 | Slave-holding landowners 369 | Nonslave-holding landowners 485 |
Acres owned	Percentage of owners	Percentage of owners	Percentage of owners	Percentage of owners
1–50	4.73	13.77	3.79	15.05
51–100	9.83	23.98	9.49	22.27
101–200	24.08	31.33	22.76	30.93
201–300	19.23	11.29	22.76	9.48
301–400	10.27	4.31	10.84	6.19
401–500	9.48	2.09	8.67	2.47
501–1,000	13.39	3.05	14.63	1.86
1,001–5,000	5.63	1.25	4.34	1.03
Above 5,000	.55	.15	.27	.21
Not determined	2.81	8.78	2.44	10.52

Thus it appears from the tables on the sizes of landholdings that most of the slaveholders and nonslaveholders owned less than 500 acres of land. In 1860 about 55 per cent of the slaveholders of Tennessee owned from 100 to 400 acres. In the bluegrass basin about 60 per cent, and in West Tennessee over 50 per cent held this amount of land. About

TABLE LXXXIV

MIDDLE TENNESSEE—BLUEGRASS BASIN

Sizes of Holdings

	BLUEGRASS BASIN AS A WHOLE, 1850		MAURY COUNTY 1850	
	Slave-holding landowners 3,297	Nonslave-holding landowners 2,266	Slave-holding landowners 843	Nonslave-holding landowners 453
Acres owned	Percentage of owners	Percentage of owners	Percentage of owners	Percentage of owners
1–50	8.56	24.04	7.00	24.94
51–100	15.58	30.07	16.37	35.32
101–200	32.03	25.40	33.57	26.49
201–300	18.34	6.15	17.91	6.18
301–400	9.96	2.41	9.73	2.65
401–500	4.76	1.21	5.34	.88
501–1,000	7.30	1.17	7.59	.88
1,001–5,000	2.37	.60	2.25	.66
Above 5,000	.06	—	—	—
Not determined	1.04	8.91	.24	1.99

40 per cent of the nonslaveholders of the state owned from 100 to 400 acres. In East Tennessee about 53 per cent of the landowning nonslaveholders had 100 to 400 acres, and on the highland rim about 46 per cent fell in this class.

Tables LXXXVIII, LXXXIX, XC, and XCI, on pages 228–29, give an analysis of slaveholdings in these sample

TABLE LXXXV

MIDDLE TENNESSEE—BLUEGRASS BASIN

Sizes of Holdings

| | BLUEGRASS BASIN AS A WHOLE, 1860 | | MAURY COUNTY 1860 | |
	Slave-holding landowners 3,292	Nonslave-holding landowners 2,873	Slave-holding landowners 986	Nonslave-holding landowners 704
Acres owned	Percentage of owners	Percentage of owners	Percentage of owners	Percentage of owners
1–50	6.73	21.01	6.90	26.99
51–100	11.01	24.54	10.45	22.73
101–200	31.59	25.92	31.95	25.43
201–300	19.43	6.92	17.75	9.52
301–400	10.69	2.22	10.85	2.84
401–500	6.34	.83	7.40	1.42
501–1,000	8.92	.85	10.65	1.56
1,001–5,000	2.29	.21	3.65	.28
Above 5,000	.14	.03	.40	.14
Not determined	2.86	17.47	—	9.09

counties. In 1860 over 97 per cent of the slaveholders in East Tennessee owned from 1 to 20 slaves. On the highland rim, in Middle Tennessee, and West Tennessee respectively, 92, 90, and 76 per cent of the slaveholders had from 1 to 20 slaves. But 85 per cent of the slaveholders in East Tennessee, 77 per cent on the highland rim, 69 per cent in

TABLE LXXXVI

West Tennessee

Sizes of Holdings

	WEST TENNESSEE AS A WHOLE, 1850		HAYWOOD COUNTY 1850	
	Slave-holding landowners 2,119	Nonslave-holding landowners 1,916	Slave-holding landowners 500	Nonslave-holding landowners 256
Acres owned	Percentage of owners	Percentage of owners	Percentage of owners	Percentage of owners
1–50	3.82	17.39	3.00	17.97
51–100	11.70	29.30	10.80	26.17
101–200	28.49	30.44	26.60	33.98
201–300	18.50	7.80	19.60	8.98
301–400	10.75	2.08	11.40	.78
401–500	6.71	1.70	5.80	2.34
501–1,000	13.09	1.31	15.80	1.17
1,001–5,000	5.08	.48	6.40	—
Above 5,000	.37	—	—	—
Not determined	1.49	9.50	.60	8.59

the bluegrass basin, and 57 per cent in West Tennessee had from 1 to 10 slaves. The pattern of slaveownership corresponds to that of landownership so that one reaches the conclusion that in Tennessee as in the lower South the bulk of slaveholders owned fewer than ten slaves, just as ap-

TABLE LXXXVII

WEST TENNESSEE

Sizes of Holdings

	WEST TENNESSEE AS A WHOLE, 1860		HAYWOOD COUNTY 1860	
	Slave-holding landowners 2,405	Nonslave-holding landowners 1,960	Slave-holding landowners 573	Nonslave-holding landowners 336
Acres owned	Percentage of owners	Percentage of owners	Percentage of owners	Percentage of owners
1–50	5.19	21.08	4.19	23.81
51–100	10.18	24.98	8.03	27.38
101–200	26.31	26.04	23.56	28.27
201–300	16.08	6.87	14.31	4.46
301–400	10.57	2.35	10.47	2.38
401–500	6.87	1.30	7.33	1.19
501–1,000	13.27	1.42	16.75	1.19
1,001–5,000	6.43	.72	10.30	1.49
Above 5,000	5.01	15.24	5.06	9.83

proximately the same group had from 100 to 400 acres of land. Thus it appears from the sample counties in the upper South and lower South that the majority of slaveholders and nonslaveholders in the regions examined were farmers falling in the same general economic groups.

TABLE LXXXVIII

SLAVEHOLDING

Grainger County

Slaves owned	1850 Slaveholders 165 Percentage of owners	1860 Slaveholders 167 Percentage of owners
1–5	62.42	62.28
6–10	21.82	22.75
11–20	12.12	11.98
21–30	3.03	2.40
31–40	.61	.60
41–50	—	—
51–100	—	—

TABLE LXXXIX

SLAVEHOLDING

Franklin County

Slaves owned	1850 Slaveholders 400 Percentage of owners	1860 Slaveholders 409 Percentage of owners
1–5	52.50	54.76
6–10	20.75	22.25
11–20	20.00	15.40
21–30	4.50	5.13
31–40	1.25	1.71
41–50	.50	.73
51–100	.50	—

TABLE XC

SLAVEHOLDING

Sumner County

Slaves owned	1850 Slaveholders 789 Percentage of owners	1860 Slaveholders 707 Percentage of owners
1–5	45.50	44.55
6–10	26.11	25.18
11–20	18.12	21.22
21–30	6.21	5.66
31–40	1.90	1.27
41–50	1.14	.99
51–100	.89	.99
101–150	.13	.14

TABLE XCI

SLAVEHOLDING

Haywood County

Slaves owned	1850 Slaveholders 610 Percentage of owners	1860 Slaveholders 610 Percentage of owners
1–5	40.00	35.57
6–10	19.68	21.48
11–20	21.80	19.67
21–30	8.36	10.49
31–40	4.10	3.28
41–50	2.13	3.93
51–100	3.77	4.59
101–150	.16	.66
151–200	—	—
201–250	—	.33

Index